"But at the end, if we are brave enough to love, if we are strong enough to forgive, if we are generous enough to rejoice in another's happiness, and if we are wise enough to know that there is enough love to go around for us all, then we can achieve a fulfillment that no other living creature will ever know…"
   Rabbi Harold S. Kushner

"The sweetness of a mother's love
comes with a few
Loving strings."
   Sandy Morrison, September 2022

SHEILA
"THERE'S NO USE CRYING OVER SPILT MILK"

PAMELA MORRISON

Copyright © 2023 PAMELA MORRISON

All rights reserved. No part of this publication may be reproduced, distributed, or transmitted in any form or by any means, including photocopying, recording, or other electronic or mechanical methods, without the prior written permission of the publisher, except in the case of brief quotations embodied in critical reviews and certain other noncommercial uses permitted by copyright law.

(✽) greenhill

https://greenhillpublishing.com.au/

Morrison, Pamela (author)
SHEILA: "There's no use crying over spilt milk"
ISBN 978-0-6456368-0-2
BIOGRAPHY

Typeset Minion Pro 11/15
Edited by Lynne Lloyd, www.lloydmosspublishing.com
Cover and book design by Green Hill

Dedicated with love to my mother Sheila,
who taught me to be brave.

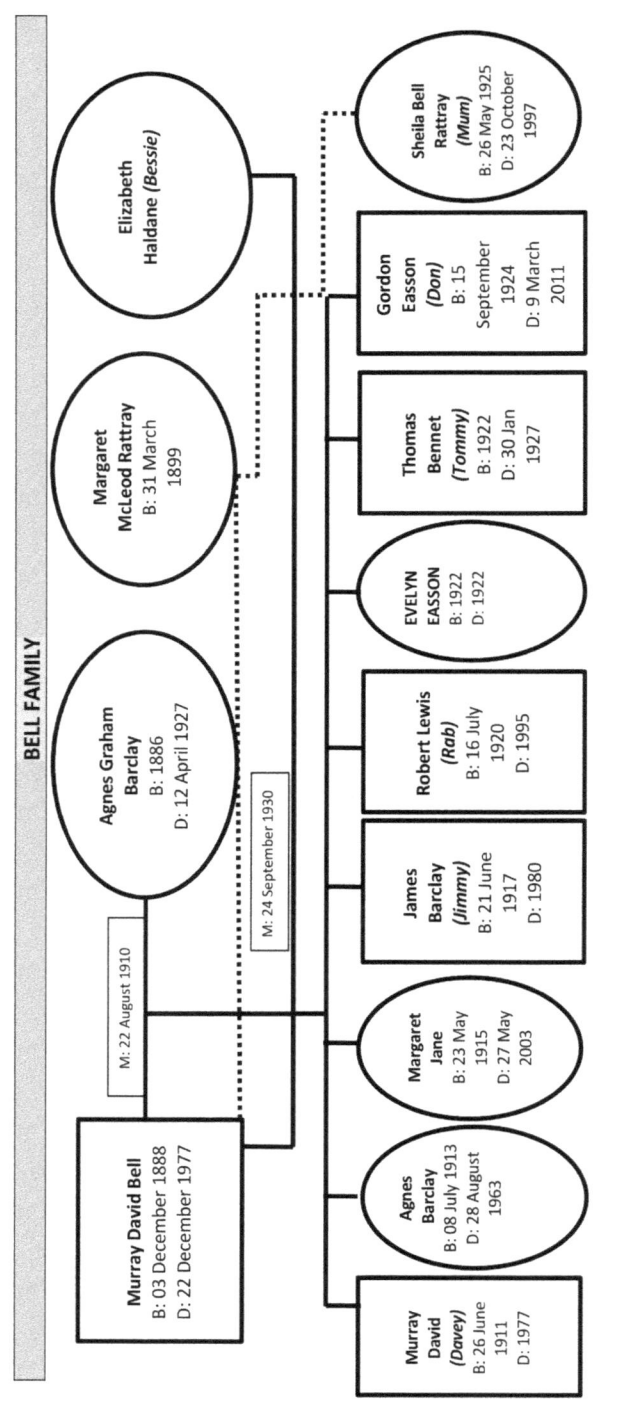

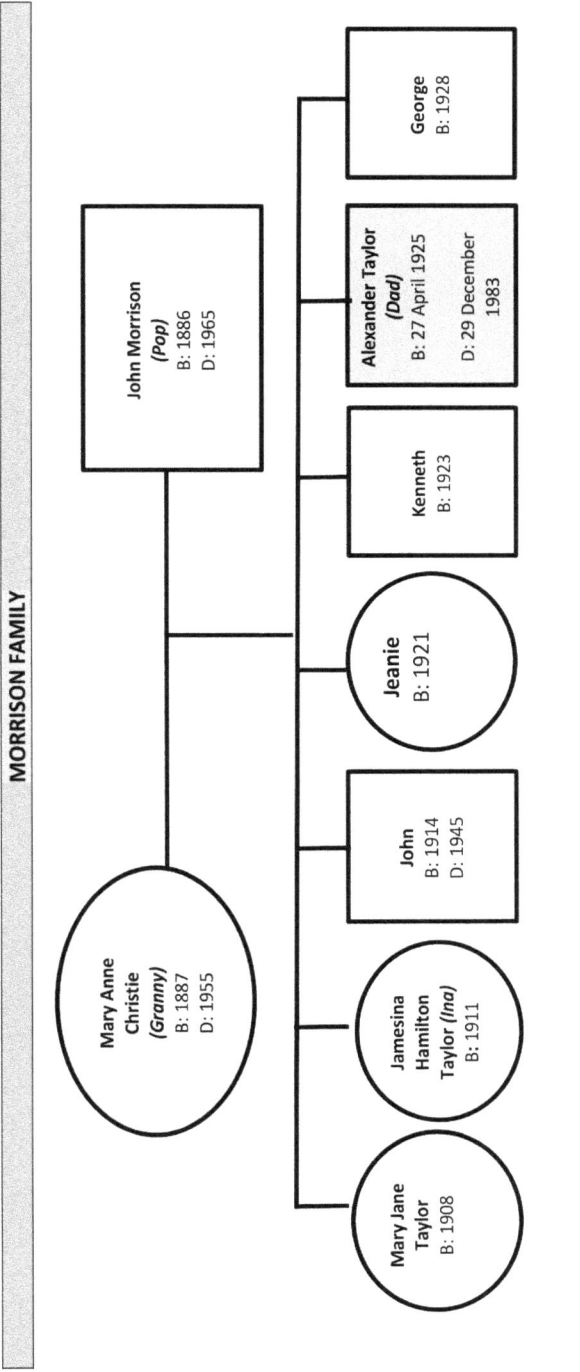

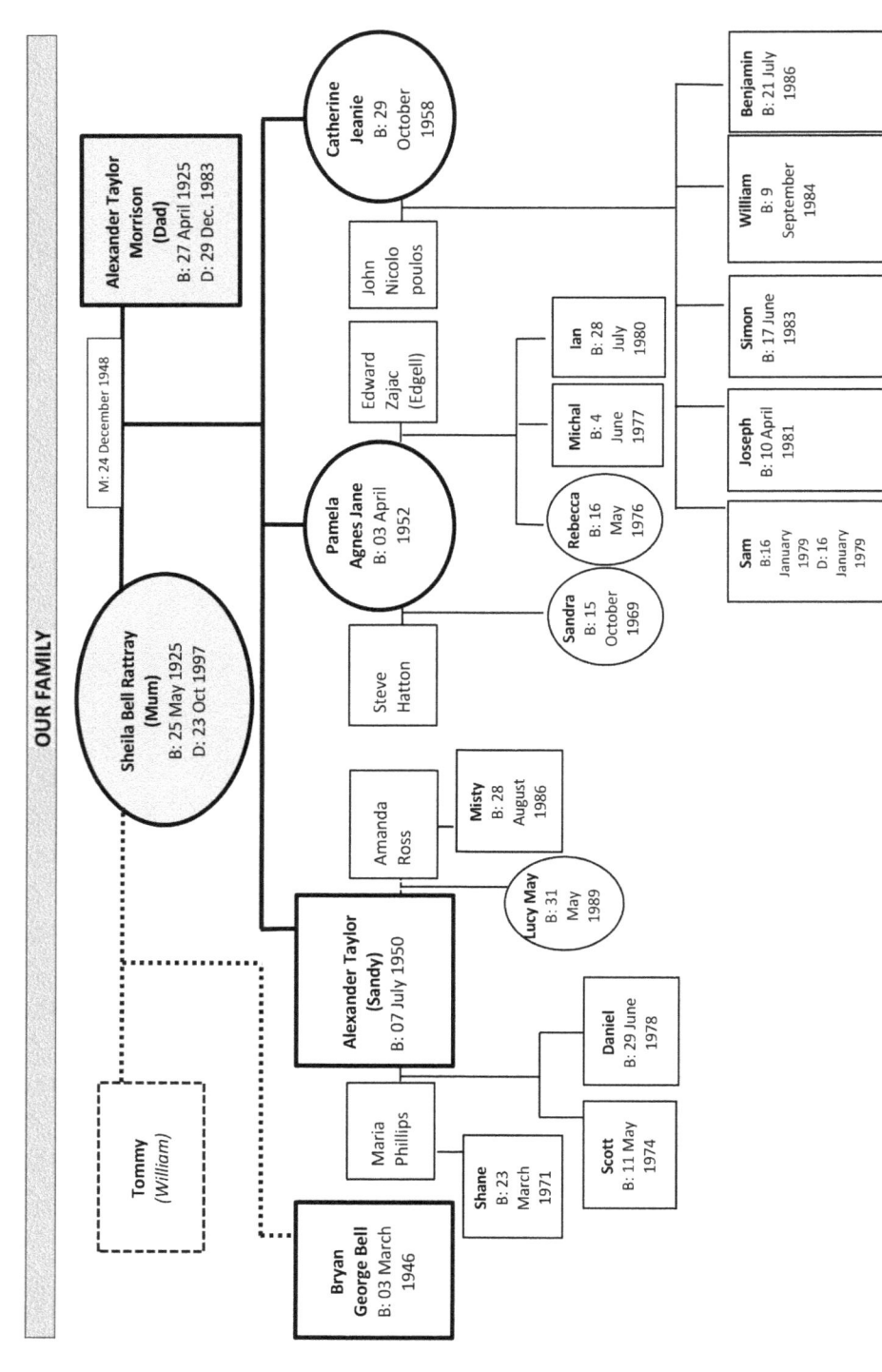

CONTENTS

Prologue 1

Chapter One: Summer 1925 7
Chapter Two: 1925 - 1927 19
Chapter Three: 1928 29
Chapter Four: 1929 36
Chapter Five: 1930 - 1936 45
Chapter Six: 1936 56
Chapter Seven: 1937 63
Chapter Eight: 1937-1938 74
Chapter Nine: 1939 82
Chapter Ten: 1940 - 1943 98
Chapter Eleven: 1943 - 1945 105
Chapter Twelve: 1945 120
Chapter Thirteen: 1946 134
Chapter Fourteen: 1947 150

Chapter Fifteen: 1948	159
Chapter Sixteen: 1949 – 1951	177
Chapter Seventeen: 1952	186
Chapter Eighteen: 1953 – 1956	202
Chapter Nineteen: 1957	212
Chapter Twenty: 1958 – 1964	218
Chapter Twenty One: 1964 – 1967	229
Chapter Twenty Two: 1968-1978	243
Chapter Twenty Three: 1978 - 1980	253
Chapter Twenty Four: 1980 – 1988	260
Chapter Twenty Five: 1988 - 1998	277
Chapter Twenty Six: 1997	288
Acknowledgments	302
Glossary	304

PROLOGUE

In the years following my mother's death, I gave little thought to the black plastic folder stored away with her photographs and papers. Within the folder nestled forty odd sheets of paper, now yellowed with age, which Mum had used to tell the story of her lifelong struggle to overcome the horrific abuse she suffered as a child and young woman. Although she had shared a little of her early life with me and my siblings over the years, I was unprepared for the emotions which overwhelmed me on reading her work for the first time.

After her death, the tattered foolscap folder was stored away in a box and hidden from sight, but it called to me from time to time; too important to be forgotten. The day arrived when, rather reluctantly, I dusted it off and sat down with a cup of tea to begin reading through it again.

I found it impossible to read about her painful struggles and victories without being haunted by the need to share her story of courage, determination, and the ability she mustered from inside herself to defy the odds stacked against her. Her story demanded to be aired in the hope it might encourage others who have suffered as she did.

Time sped by, as a busy life does, until eventually I retired from my demanding full-time career, pulled myself together, and sat down with the folder in front of me. Inhaling deeply, and sending up a quick prayer for courage, I began my journey.

Carefully opening the plastic cover of the folder to the first page, Mum's well remembered writing jumped out at me and I let my mind wander. I imagined her sitting at the laminate dining table in her home in Elizabeth Park, South Australia, staring into the past and seeking a way to begin writing her story. The sunlight would be slanting through the window, revealing the grey roots in her dark, permed hair; sadly, I was usually a little late making time to dye it for her. In this image, I could see an unusually deep frown form between her deep blue eyes, as she became lost in her memories, her mind travelling back over her sixty years on Earth and touching down on moments in time.

I notice her suddenly flinching and blinking, bringing herself back to her writing task. She picks up the pen sitting next to her cup of tea and returns to her difficult mission. I held this picture of her in my mind as I absorbed the words she had poured out onto the first page: *"The first thing I can remember is feeling different to the others."*

She commenced the monumental task of releasing her long-held secret pain onto the pages before her on the advice of her minister after sharing a little of her story with him. The Reverend had gently spoken to her of how the very act of laying a painful story on paper can help a person to process and release their stories. He also suggested it may help her to find forgiveness for herself as well as others or, at the very least, make peace with the past.

Following Dad's sudden death when he was only fifty-eight, Mum's grief had overwhelmed her, leaving her raw, bleeding, and slowly suffocating under the burden of her sorrow. While in that dark place, she found herself experiencing sudden flashbacks to her childhood and had sought out the Reverend for help. It had taken great courage for her to finally speak out about the many secrets she had locked away inside her soul for a lifetime.

As I turn the pages, her struggle to lay down some of her memories becomes obvious as, on occasion, she appears to have made several attempts to describe an incident, evidenced by the various shades of ink which are poured, or sometimes hurled in a rage, across the page. Also, some of her recollections seem to have come to her out of synch, causing her to write these on small scraps of paper and attach them in the correct place with a tiny gold safety pin. As my mind searched for the woman I simply knew as 'Mum' within the devastating trauma I was absorbing, I noticed her words sometimes came to a screeching halt. I could feel that the pain had become unbearable at that point, as some words are underscored again and again in a fury, occasionally tearing the delicate paper.

The process of composing those pages, unlocking and processing the memories, along with the emotions bound to them, proved to be cathartic for her and my siblings and I watched her eventually emerge from the overwhelming darkness. She found hope in understanding that the decision to forgive may release her from the emotions which were harming her.

I believe she tried every day to forgive her father and, perhaps more importantly, herself. That decision alone gave her some peace, allowing the following few years of her life to be happy ones for her.

I have used Mum's writing as a guide to my research and blended her words with my memories, the memories of my siblings and the stories and information my dear cousins have shared with me. I have taken a little creative licence in the following pages, adding some history and background, to Mum's own writing.

It has taken many years and tears, hours of research and countless sporadic writing attempts to reach a point where I must let her story go. Writing this book has helped me understand the complexities of the woman who was just 'Mum' to the kids she raised.

I am awestruck by the way she managed to raise three children without inflicting untold damage on us, as we hear so often that child abuse is frequently intergenerational. In any case, Mum managed to turn the tide and raised well-adjusted human beings; at least my siblings and I think we're OK … kind of anyway! She was a woman with great strength of character, and I hope her story will encourage other victims of abuse to seize back the power stolen from them by their abusers, and enable them to view themselves as champions, overcomers, and masters of their future.

CHAPTER ONE

SUMMER 1925

The weak morning sun nudged through a small window in the stairwell spreading a little light around the dim landing. Although it was the middle of summer, the harshness of a Scottish winter never entirely relinquishes its hold on cold concrete stairs. Eventually, the rays of sunlight crept along the icy floor to a coir doormat on the second story landing and reached a large, brown cardboard shoe box containing a tiny, sleeping baby.

When the sun reached the babe's eyes, she blinked, yawned and felt her belly twist with hunger. Filling her lungs, she began crying for a feed, her bellows soon echoing around the stairwell and getting more strident by the second.

Suddenly, the glossy door behind the doormat swished open to reveal a tall, slim figure, frowning in consternation. The woman, Mrs Agnes Bell, swept back the dark hair threatening to escape it's clasp and gasped as she peered down at the box containing the source of the noise. Bending down a little, she looked more closely at the wee red-faced tyke who, with sweaty dark hair plastered to her head, continued to scream her indignation to the world.

Straightening up, the harassed woman glanced around the landing for the baby's mother but there was no one there. She stepped across the box to peer over the iron banisters calling out … *"hello, is there anyone there?"* The sound merged with the baby's cries and echoed off the walls, but her query remained unanswered as the stairwell was inhabited only by herself and the babe.

As a capable, kindly woman with a brood of children of her own, she acted on her maternal instinct and scooped the box up, closing the door behind her. She walked into the kitchen and placed the awkward makeshift bed gently down on the floor beside the warm cooking range. Easing herself into the familiar low chair she used for nursing, she gave a deep sigh and looked down at the baby. Carefully lifting the squalling bairn into her arms, she rummaged around in the soft blankets for a bottle of milk but came up frustratingly empty handed.

With the cries becoming ever louder, she worried about her baby son waking up, he had been so fractious last night, keeping her up for hours; she had to do something quickly! Seeing nothing else for it, she sighed deeply, opened the bodice of her housedress, and put the baby to her breast where the little one greedily began to suckle, ah… instant peace!

Relieved the baby was now content, she found many unanswered questions running riot through her mind; who was this wee one's mother, where was she and why had she left the baby on her particular doorstep when there were three other doors on the landing? Was she ill, in trouble, homeless, desperate?

She wondered whether the mother was unmarried and suffering financial problems which would make it impossible to care for a baby while working. However, there were plenty of orphanages in the area where she could have left the baby. Honestly, she huffed, I have enough to contend with, caring for a house full of children and an often-angry husband!

Pondering on her husband's anger, which was unleashed on the older children as well as herself at times, she worried about how he would react to finding this tiny intruder in his house. She considered sending one of the children to the shop he managed to inform him of the strange situation; he could call the authorities from the shop telephone and ask them to come to the house to collect the baby. She swiftly decided against that course of action as he would very likely become angry with whichever child she sent.

As the baby suckled contentedly, her thoughts wandered to her younger days when she was courted by the courteous, attractive Murray David Bell. She remembered the hope she had once held for the future as a blushing new bride, hope which was stifled within the first few years of marriage.

She had grown up in a well-respected family in Glasgow, and when she first met David, as he preferred to be called, he had appeared to be a man on the 'up and up.' He held himself with an almost military bearing, giving the appearance of a man who was much taller than his actual stature. He was charismatic and somewhat handsome, a dapper dresser, and a perfect gentleman throughout their courtship.

He managed a shoe store called Saxone, in the High Street of a small town on the east coast of Scotland. Saxone was a large company which manufactured shoes in its Scottish factory, selling them through more than 100 branches across the country. The company offered abundant prospects for advancement and, as an ambitious man, his dreams of owning a store beckoned.

Her parents adored him, as he had delighted them thoroughly, but her two down-to-earth older sisters were wary of his good looks and charm, unconvinced by what they perceived to be a facade. They believed she was too good for David and would be marrying beneath her if she went ahead with the wedding.

Nevertheless, ever the optimist, she was happy to be swept up by his magnetism and promising future. Their small wedding, on the 22nd of August 1910 was just perfect. Afterwards, as they boarded the train to be carried across Scotland, she eagerly turned her mind towards the future and her new home.

David had been thrilled when his first son and namesake, Murray David, whom they called Davey for short, arrived a short ten months after the wedding. Davey's birth was followed two years later by the arrival of baby Agnes, who shared her mother's name as tradition demanded. Their marriage seemed to be on a good, solid path. Sadly, during the following years, David's business ambitions did not materialise as he wished. The Great War and the following worldwide depression had a huge economic impact across the globe, leading to downturns in every business. His thwarted ambitions changed him; her dapper, likeable young husband slowly transformed into a man beset with frustration and anger.

With the arrival of a new baby every two years, David's behaviour became extremely erratic, and the family suffered from his bouts of brutal rage. At the time of Mum's arrival, the household was filled to the brim with seven children: Davey 14, Agnes 12, Margaret 10, Jimmy 8, Rab 5, Tommy 3, and 9 month old Gordon.

Noticing the baby had stopped suckling and was fast asleep, the busy woman was brought abruptly back to the moment. She tucked the beautiful hand-knitted shawl around the baby tightly, stood up and popped the bundle carefully down on the chair, surprised by how tiny and light it was. Crouching down, she rummaged through the large box more carefully, seeking clues as to where and with whom this foundling belonged.

While taking the clothes and blankets out one by one, she couldn't help noticing the fine needlework in each small, soft item. The hand stitching and embroidery were so delicate, and the teeny jackets were exquisitely knitted; this was obviously no poverty-stricken streetwalker's baby! Finally, the box was empty apart from a blanket on the bottom, so she lifted that out too, and spotted what looked to be an official document underneath, carefully folded.

A glint of excitement in her eyes, she snatched it up and unfolded it carefully. She realised the paper she was looking at was the baby's birth certificate and knew this could be helpful to the authorities. The birth date was noted as 26 May

1925 – around six weeks ago; this baby was only eight months younger than her youngest son Gordon, who was affectionately called Don. Her eyes skimmed down the page coming across the baby's Christian name, Sheila - so it was a girl, no surprise there as her small, delicate, features had suggested as much.

Her eyes raced across to snatch up the next piece of information. What she read on the paper made her hand come up of its own accord to clamp over her mouth, muffling the sob which threatened to explode, as she spotted her own married name in bold ink.

Confused and unable to decipher the document further as it was clutched in her shaking hand, she stood up and laid it out on the table, flattening it between her clenched fists. Taking a deep breath to calm herself, she tried again, but saw there had been no mistake, this child had been given the middle name of Bell.

Reading on, she saw the mother was recorded as Margaret McLeod Rattray. She remembered Margaret, the attractive young woman who had been an assistant in David's shop. She had mysteriously disappeared just before the autumn sales last year, sending David into the devil of a rage for days. Understanding came crashing in on her and she took a step back, distancing herself from the paper! This doorstep was chosen because her husband, the father of her own children, had also sired this baby.

Shocked to her core, she left the baby asleep in the comfortable box and went about her morning chores in a daze. It was the beginning of the school holidays and there were plenty of little helpers around to care for Don and Sheila when they woke up; they were all excited about the surprising new arrival, particularly Agnes and Margaret. She cooked the midday meal as usual and waited for her husband to step through the door at 12.05 sharp, as he always did.

The waiting seemed interminable, and she was so afraid. What would David do when she confronted him with this offspring of his, an unwanted intrusion into the house? Would he beat her or hurt baby Sheila or any of the other children in his rage? She knew from painful experience that when he was enraged, he was beyond reason. What was to be done?

When David arrived home tired and hungry, he washed up and went straight into the parlour, his private sanctuary, as usual. He ate all his meals alone in the parlour, served on a wooden tray with a clean tray cloth and napkin. One of the children was generally required to bring the meal, and the unlucky child would do so with apprehension and trembling knees. After giving him enough time to finish his meal, Mrs Bell smoothed her hair down and approached the door carrying the birth certificate in trembling hands and knocked.

David, who was reading the morning newspaper, wasn't too pleased at being interrupted; nevertheless, she sat down at the table without speaking and placed the birth certificate before him. At first, he was puzzled as to why she was laying what appeared to be an important document before him but replaced his glasses on his nose and picked the document up. Squinting, he read through the document carefully, a deep frown forming between his eyes. Silence ensued for a few moments before he looked over at her calmly and coldly saying *"And what does this have to do with you?"*

Hesitating for a moment, she quietly explained about her unexpected find on the doorstep that morning. His eyes blazed at her for a second before he stood and shouted at her, spittle flying in all directions, demanding to know where the baby was. Without waiting for a reply, he rushed from the room with her following him, trying to clutch his arm to stop him before he did something terrible. He stormed across the hall and into the kitchen, coming to a sudden halt before the improvised bed, staring down at his baby daughter.

After what felt like hours but was probably only moments, he roused himself, grabbed the box, and stormed out of the house without a word. Standing rooted to the spot in his wake, a whirlwind of emotions flying around her head, she worried about what would become of the innocent baby girl. She finally shook herself out of her reverie and began her normal chores, however it didn't take long before the fear crept into her mind: what would happen when David arrived home?

Entering the parlour to clear the abandoned dishes from David's meal, she noticed the baby's birth certificate was still on the table. She picked the offending document up and placed it in his walnut roll-top desk, unsure if it was the right thing to do; she didn't want any of the children to see it.

David returned later in the evening. He came strutting through the front door at his usual time, washed up and entered the parlour, as was his normal habit, and waited for his evening meal. She entered the room, fear gripping her throat, and asked him what he had done with the little one. He completely ignored her, staring straight ahead as though she was not even there.

What could she do but retreat? It was as if he had decided this daughter of his did not exist. She had borne a brood of children to this man and relied on him to feed and clothe them all. It was impossible to leave! She was too afraid to press him for answers or express her pain at this final humiliation. Instead, she decided to assume he had taken the baby home to her mother, having no choice but to let the matter rest there for the sake of her family.

The older children discovered much later that their father had taken the baby, along with her fine clothing, to a family who lived in a village close by. She remained there for almost three years.

Such was the story of Sheila's calamitous arrival into the Bell family. That unwelcome baby grew up to become my mother, and her father, David, eventually became my grandfather. It was through the older children, Davey, Agnes, and Margaret, who were old enough at the time to remember the drama, that Mum later heard this story. It must surely have been an unforgettable event in their lives.

***

When my siblings, Sandy, Cathy and I had grown up, Mum told us the story of her birth and uninvited arrival into the Bell house. There had been rumours in the family over the years that she had been born in a Salvation Army home and those whispers provided me with a great starting point for my research. According to Salvation Army records, when Mum was born, Margaret was staying at Seafield House which was their mother and baby home in Dundee on the East coast of Scotland.

She left the home only six weeks after giving birth, which was far earlier than women were usually released as they were required to remain there until they had worked off the debts incurred during their stay. The records show she had been summoned home to care for her own mother who had become very ill. This early release would have been achieved by her family paying their daughter's debts in full, but it would be unlikely the summons included a welcome for her little illegitimate daughter.

I have often thought about Agnes Bell, the mother of Mum's half siblings, and of her kindness towards a little foundling on that summer morning. Despite the shock her arrival would have caused, she did her best for Mum; she was obviously a warm and loving mother to her children. Mum's photograph box contains two photos of her, which show her as an attractive, rather refined woman with dark hair and a strong, determined set to her chin.

In the earliest photograph taken in 1914, she sits by her husband with her baby daughter Agnes on her knee and her little son Davey at her side. She appears healthy, proud, and gracious in a light-coloured dress with a slight secret smile playing on her lips. Her eyes seem to sparkle as she gazes into the camera, her head at a confident angle. Her proud looking husband stands behind his family, looking rather dashing with his bow tie and straw hat, his oval face serious and his eyes boring into the camera.

The second photograph, taken only four years later in 1918, tells a quite different story. She sits with baby Jimmy on her knee, a scowling Davey on her left, and an equally scowling Agnes on her right and little Margaret, who was around two years old at the time, peers inquisitively into the camera.

Apart from the addition of two more children, the biggest change in those years is in her appearance, the secret smile has vanished. Her face appears longer, and her expression is grim; in fact, her general demeanour is of a very different woman indeed. The image conveys the impression that life had taken a severe toll on her in those four short years.

Mum's birth mother, Margaret McLeod Rattray, remains a mystery. All that is known about her is that she was an assistant in her father's shop and devastatingly, despite searching as hard as she could, or could afford to in the pre-Internet days, Mum was never able to find her. She remained as shadowy and unsubstantial as a wraith for the rest of Mum's life.

Despite the advantages of the information age, my own searches have only been able to find records of Margaret's own parents, Henry and Catherine Rattray and go no further than her marriage to a man named James Mason in 1933. As the trail appears to end at this point, I wonder if they migrated overseas at some stage.

One can't help but wonder about Margaret's thoughts as she lay her daughter into the box and placed it carefully down, turning to walk quickly away. Did she think leaving her baby girl on David Bell's doorstep was the best thing for her, or was she in such a desperate state she felt she had no other choice? Did she look back with tears streaming down her face as she ran out of the building? Did she come to regret her decision later in her life? Perhaps she believed her debonair boss would be a good father as he appeared to be such a family man.

Apparently, my grandfather was a real charmer when he wanted to be, and I wonder about Mum's beginnings; was she born out of a love affair, a quick fumble in the stockroom or, more troubling, was she coerced or bullied into having sex with him? All the 'maybes' and 'what ifs' must have crowded Mum's mind throughout her life. Unfortunately, these questions will forever remain unanswered.

CHAPTER TWO

1925 - 1927

In the months following Mum's shocking arrival and prompt disappearance, Agnes Bell's health began to fail. It seems likely that, after working so hard to be a good mother and wife for fifteen years despite David's black moods and violence towards her and the children, the appearance of his illegitimate child had broken her spirit.

She struggled on through the following months to care for her home and family. She had been a strong and capable woman and loving mother but the constant drain on her body and mind took a heavy toll. The Great Depression was having a bad effect on the business, adding to her husband's stress, and making his temper even shorter than before.

In the past, she had been able to protect her children from his worst beatings by pushing in between David and the child who was the subject of his wrath, but as her strength waned the beatings became worse and life for the older children became even more difficult. Her cruel husband would sometimes drag an errant child into the outdoor laundry and lock the door before delivering his beating as she stood, screaming and banging her fists on the wooden door, begging him to stop.

Her inability to protect her children weighed heavily on her mind. Davey, as the eldest son, was particularly protective of his mother and often stood up to his father to defend her, which of course meant he received the wrath which was meant for her as well as the beating he was due to receive for his audacity.

The children tried their best to help her, especially when it became obvious over time that she was terribly ill. Davey was rapidly becoming a young man and, at fourteen years old, began working. At twelve, Agnes was her eldest girl and a great help around the house, as was Margaret. The youngest children, Jimmy, Rab, Tommy and little Don still needed her care, and the cooking, cleaning and laundry exhausted her. Before long, she developed a constant cough which often kept her awake during the night, sometimes even bringing up blood, and she suffered from high fevers at times. Each coughing fit left her totally washed out and, although she had always been slim, she was now very thin and scraggly looking. Discovering yet another skirt, petticoat or bloomers that she had to pin closed each morning, she would sigh and consign it to the ever-growing mending pile for alteration.

She struggled on, but eventually the day arrived when she was so exhausted no amount of willpower could get her out of bed. Agnes came into the room in the morning to find her mother delirious and burning up with fever. She sent Margaret to a neighbour who had a telephone to ask her to ring the doctor before organising the rest of the children, sending the older boys off to school.

When the doctor arrived and saw their mother's condition, he immediately sent Agnes to call for an ambulance. When it arrived, she and her sister stood at the bedroom door with the little ones crowded around them, mouths agape. Together they watched their mother, swathed in a red blanket, being carried out of the house on a stretcher. She disappeared into the back of the ambulance which sped off, bells jangling loudly in the cold morning air, leaving them alone.

As they watched the ambulance disappear around the corner, the children clustered closer to their big sisters, stunned and frightened. They were all afraid: what would happen to them now? Agnes, being the eldest girl, took charge and sent Margaret to the shop to let their father know what had happened. Ushering the children back into the house, she thought of the myriad of chores waiting to be done and set to work organising the household.

When their father came home later in the evening, he summoned Davey and Agnes to the parlour and told them their mother was now in Ochil Hills Sanatorium in Perth as she was suffering from Pulmonary Tuberculosis. This news was terrifying for the children as they had heard of TB before and knew of friends who had lost family members to the dreaded disease. He told Agnes she was to leave school straight away to take care of the house and children, an order which devastated her, as she was a smart and curious child who enjoyed school. He said Margaret was to stay at school but help in the house when she came home. Later, he warned the other children to pay attention to what their biggest sister said and obey her completely, or else...

The children were alone, motherless, and terrified. The younger ones only understood that their mother was very sick and in hospital, and they were to follow orders and do their chores. None of the children expected to see their mother again. Their father was gone all day, returning home at 12.05pm sharp for midday dinner and then heading back to work, only returning late at night when the younger children were in bed. His late nights were a relief for the children, as without their father around, they were safe from danger.

Most of the household tasks fell to Agnes and Margaret, who were only children themselves, and they were careful to obey their father to the letter. One of the hard and fast rules which proved difficult for them and for little Don was that the wee lad MUST NOT be allowed to go to bed before his father came home at night to see him. The poor toddler would sit in his highchair, fighting off sleep, but although the girls felt sorry for him, they knew better than to disobey.

One night, Don was in his highchair by the kitchen fire as usual while Margaret was ironing, and Agnes was preparing the porridge to steep for next morning when Don, falling into a sound sleep, tumbled out of the highchair and smashed his head on the steel fender around the fireplace. Of course, he instantly began to scream blue murder, just as their father came through the front door. He rushed into the kitchen and grabbed the boy from Margaret's arms and held him close until he fell asleep. The girls knew they were in for it and were quivering when he came back to the kitchen after putting Don in his cot.

He screamed at them, calling them lazy good for nothing besoms and lashed out at them, fists flying. Margaret received a terrible beating with a stick that night; she was usually the one who bore the worst of his rage. Agnes managed to avoid most of the flailing stick and kept her distance until his temper eventually subsided and he stormed off. From this time on, the girls made sure they tied a belt around Don when they placed him in the highchair.

Life was exceedingly difficult for the family during this time; the Great Depression was having a brutal effect across the country. Most people didn't have money to buy new shoes and instead were stuffing their old ones with newspaper and cardboard to make them last a bit longer. Of course, these thrifty ideas meant the shop's sales were declining, leaving their father more stressed and angrier than ever. He gave the girls money for the housekeeping, but the amount continued to dwindle each week.

The poor children lived totally on their nerves, walking on eggshells whenever their father was around. Agnes and Margaret had to contend with his habit of coming into the house and walking around, inspecting their housekeeping. He would enter a room and slide his fingers along the furniture looking for dust, and God help those girls if he found any. It was as though he was deliberately trying to find a reason to allow his wrath to explode.

The four eldest worked hard to stretch each precious penny as far as it would go but there was barely enough for food, let alone new clothes for the children. The girls learned to make meals which were filling for the children, but their father always had to have a decent midday meal, regardless of the leanness of the pantry. They became quite clever in their efforts and would often send either Davey or Jimmy trudging all the way to the neighbouring village to buy something such as flour by the pound and carry it home in a paper bag. They would put the flour into the old, more expensive packaging so their father wouldn't know, and keep the extra few pennies saved for something else.

Margaret and Davey would often steal coal from the coal yard and once or twice, they even stole some of the horsehair stuffing out of the chaise lounge in the parlour and sold it to the rag and bone man. They stuffed the gap left by their thievery with old rags. Sometimes, the children were lucky enough to grab a tray of two-day-old buns early in the morning from the local baker who felt sorry for them. They would hide the tray under one of the beds and share them out after school, before their father came home.

One momentous afternoon, an ambulance arrived outside the door. Agnes and Margaret answered the knock and were stunned to see their mother being helped up the wooden stairs by the ambulance men. They threw the door wide open, hardly able to believe their eyes. Each taking an arm and bubbling over with joy, they brought her into the hallway just as their father came out of the parlour. He told them to make their mother comfortable, before he headed back to the shop.

The girls quickly set about settling her in, making a bed on the sofa for her and stoking up the fire; all the while scolding little Tommy and Don for getting under their feet. When she was settled, she told the girls she was surprised they had not been expecting her. They didn't tell her that their father hadn't let them know she was strong enough to come home. The children had not seen her for almost a year as the sanatorium did not allow visitors.

Although overjoyed to see their mother, they were dismayed to notice she was even thinner than she had been when she left home and her once abundant dark hair was now sparse and streaked with grey as though she was a much older woman, not the forty-year old they knew her to be. Hiding their unease, they made her tea and scones, and sat with her, holding her hands until she started to fall asleep, tears of joy still spilling down her cheeks.

When the rest of the children arrived home from school, they couldn't believe their eyes and threw their arms around her, crawling all over the sofa, vying for her attention. So happy to see her darling children, she couldn't help hugging them all close to her, crying all the time for joy. It felt as though she had been away for a lifetime, they had grown so much.

They all talked ten to the dozen until eventually she became exhausted, and Agnes had to order everyone out of the parlour to let her rest. When their father came home in the evening, he told the girls to bring supper for them both into the parlour. When they cleared the dishes away afterwards, the girls were troubled to see their mother had only eaten a tiny amount of soup and a few small bites of bread.

The girls spent as much time as they could with their mother, bringing her little treats and treasures to keep her spirits up and fawning over her. They kept the younger children quiet and only allowed them to have short visits with her, so she didn't get too tired, but despite all their best efforts, her condition worsened over the following week or two. She developed a very hoarse voice, struggling to even whisper and spent most of her days sleeping.

Eventually the doctor had to be summoned again and, with eyes filled with unshed tears she tried to hide from the children, she was stretchered back into an ambulance. The children heard her sobbing as it pulled away, taking her back to the sanatorium. Sometime later, their father informed the older children the TB had spread into her throat. The children were devastated.

Only a few weeks after their mother's short visit home, little four-year-old Tommy kept everyone awake all night with a fever and a horrible cough that made him vomit. Agnes called for a doctor who, on arrival, took only few moments to diagnose whooping cough. Knowing how dangerous 'the whoop' was, the girls devised a roster to make sure he was never left alone. Someone had to be constantly with him to see to his needs; nevertheless, his fever kept getting worse.

Late one evening, when Tommy had been terribly ill for over a week, it was eight-year-old Rab's turn to sit with him and he did his best to keep him cool by mopping his brow and talking about the things they would do when he was better. Eventually, Tommy slipped into what appeared to be a deep and peaceful sleep and the room was silent. Rab was beginning to nod off himself when he was startled by Tommy sitting bolt upright with a radiant smile on his flushed face, and pointing towards the corner of the room, crying out '*The angel is here*.'

Rab swiftly swivelled towards the corner to see what his brother was so animated about, but seeing nothing, turned back again only to see Tommy laying back on the bed with his eyes closed, a deathly pallor spreading over his face which had been so flushed only moments before. Rab ran to get Agnes and they both rushed back into the room as their little brother took his last breath.

What a terrible ordeal for young Rab and the children to face, especially without their mother there to comfort them. Naturally, they were distraught at losing their brother who had been taken from them so cruelly. Their father arranged the funeral but didn't say much to them; he was not one to show love to his children.

In the meantime, unknown to them, their mother was weakening further despite the fresh air she was wheeled outside to enjoy, the good food she picked at, and the medicine she was given. She missed her children terribly and fought hard to get better, obeying the doctor's orders to the letter and doing everything in her power to recover. When a letter arrived from David, informing her of Tommy's death, her profound grief took the fight right out of her, and she followed him to the grave within weeks. The children, already grieving over Tommy, were now at their lowest ebb, heartbroken and motherless.

It is hard to imagine how hard this time must have been for the children, hungry and alone, but they had no option other than to keep going and manage as best as they could, the older children caring for the younger ones. They were left to deal with their twofold grief without adult help or guidance and they supported each other as much as possible, forming the strong bonds they needed to hold them together.

Mum was still living with the foster family during this time, and therefore had no firsthand memory of this sad period. It wasn't until she was much older that her sisters told her about that horrible time. The children's aunts, their mother's sisters, who were somewhat aware of the situation in the household, were often heard to say their sister had died of a broken heart. This makes me wonder how Mum felt when she heard about Mrs Bell's early demise. Did she feel some responsibility for causing at least part of the heartbreak which, according to Mrs Bell's sisters had supposedly caused her death? It is not something that Mum ever mentioned to me.

CHAPTER THREE

1928

Despite the trauma the children endured, the older ones had not forgotten the little baby girl who had spent only one morning in their home, innocently creating such a storm. The size of the baby, compared to the bedlam her arrival had caused, was disproportionate; how could they possibly forget that fateful time? What they especially remembered was their mother's kindness towards her, caring for her as though she was her own baby, even for that short time.

It was also clear to them their father had been livid when he arrived home for his noonday meal; leaving their mother tearful and distressed when he flew out the front door in a rage, the baby's box in hand. They often wondered where the baby had gone, and what was so special yet upsetting about her.

Following his mother's death, gentle Davey, who was now a young man of sixteen, decided to set about solving the puzzle. He stole into his father's hallowed parlour and searched through his documents for clues as to her whereabouts. In the walnut roll-top desk, he found a pile of official looking envelopes and opened the first one. He quickly realised he had hit the jackpot when he found Margaret's birth certificate inside and the one underneath revealed his mother's death certificate.

With no real order to the pile, he opened them one by one until he found what he thought might be what he was looking for, a birth certificate in the name of Sheila Bell Rattray. His heart almost stopped. He was old enough to understand what this certificate meant and why that wee one had been the cause of such an uproar on the fateful morning of her arrival. Reading on, he saw the baby's mother was recorded as Margaret McLeod Rattray, the lady who had worked in his father's shop, and the baby had been born in May 1925. This fitted the time frame perfectly and he realised he and his siblings had a half-sister somewhere in the world.

At the bottom of the pile, he found an envelope addressed to his father. It contained a letter requesting '*an increase in the monthly payments for your daughter's keep.*' The writer's address was in a town only a short bus ride away, and Davey determined that, as he was the real man of the house, he would visit her to make sure she was alright. He felt certain his mother would look down from heaven and approve, so both he and Margaret went to the address.

They were not impressed with the house or the people she was staying with, it was smelly, and the woman there did not seem friendly. They saw their little half-sister only fleetingly, as she was asleep in her cot, and they had been warned not to wake her. A month later, Davey decided to visit again and was shocked to find Mum sitting on the floor wearing a dirty dress, her straight dark hair matted at the back, snot running from her nose into her mouth, unheeded.

She was playing with a rosary but looked up at him when he entered the room, her piercing blue eyes meeting his for a second, before she went back to rattling the beads. She didn't interact with him when he crouched down and spoke to her, appearing to have shut him out completely. He looked around him at the appalling conditions in the house and picked her up. He took the rosary out of her hands and threw it on the floor. Mumbling *"There's no way you're staying in this Catholic hell hole,"* he walked out of the house with her in his arms.

Davey's comments sound quite ludicrous and embarrassing in today's world, but religious sectarianism still held sway in Scotland at the time. Catholics and Protestants had been sworn enemies since the reformation of the church in the Middle Ages, with each claiming the higher ground. While growing up in Scotland, I was aware of this deep divide between us without it being specifically discussed. The belief that we, the Protestants, were at the top of the class structure, followed by Catholics and, last of all, the Gypsies was somehow entrenched.

As a child, I was aware of this division, although I don't think it affected me in any way. Sadly, this animosity is still deeply rooted in Scotland and, of course, Northern Ireland. It exists under the surface of certain sectors of society, especially football crowds, with some teams originally formed in historically Catholic areas and some in Protestant, with occasional violence erupting during or after matches.

When Davey arrived home bearing Mum in his arms proudly, very pleased with himself and sporting a silly grin, he simply said to the girls *"Say hello to our wee sister"*. The girls stared in horror at this calamity of a child coming back into the house. They were understandably terrified about what would happen when their father came home. They bathed her, washed her matted hair, dressed her in some of Don's clean clothes, and set her down on the floor to play with her brother.

When their father arrived home that night, he washed up as usual and headed for the parlour and his evening meal, also as usual. However, he came to a sudden halt at the open kitchen doorway, halfway through a stride, because he noticed the little child playing with Don. *"What the hell is that"* he roared, and the girls answered with trembling voices, *"It's our wee sister Sheila, Davey brought her home."* He flew immediately into a terrible fury and strode into the kitchen, snatched the toddler up in his arms in one fell swoop and rushed to the open kitchen window, where he attempted to dash her out.

Ever the quick thinker, Agnes grabbed her just as she was about to go over the window ledge and clutched her close to her chest, then stood firmly glaring at her father, who was rooted to the spot, seething with temper. They stood like that for a minute that seemed like hours, locked in a silent battle, before he turned and stormed out front door. The kitchen window was on the first story of the building and I'm certain Mum would not have survived the fall. When he returned later in the evening, their father acted as though nothing had happened, and he totally ignored the fact that his little daughter was in the house at all. If only he had continued to ignore her presence into the future, perhaps she would not have suffered as much as she did throughout her childhood.

I don't know what punishment Davey received, but as a strong young man, he was now able to defend himself well enough I suppose. These events began a pattern whereby Mum's siblings always did their best to safeguard and protect her, a pattern which would remain strong throughout the rest of their lives.

Since their mother had been whisked away from them, the children had developed different ways of coping with their father's violent rages. Of the boys, Davey was strong enough to defend himself, but Jimmy and Rab were much younger and suffered many horrific beatings. Agnes was feisty and haughty, and would sometimes glower back at him, showing no fear until he backed off.

Mum often spoke of her vivid memories of Agnes standing in front of the mirror above the kitchen fireplace, vigorously brushing her gorgeous auburn hair while her father thundered on at her. He would shout and work up a rage, spit flying, but she would ignore him and hastily slip away from his grasp and out through the front door, just in time to escape his fists.

Gentle Margaret on the other hand would stand like a deer in the headlights of his wrath, literally frozen in place with fear. Her terror would cause her own urine to puddle on the floor beneath her. Rooted to the spot helplessly, with her eyes squeezed tightly shut, he would seize her and begin the inevitable beating. She was often his hapless victim, being unable to move, while the other children fled for their lives.

Although corporal punishment was a normal way of disciplining children in those days with a smack on the bottom or even with a belt, switch or wooden spoon, the beatings these children regularly received went way beyond a clout around the ear or a sore bum.

As I mentioned earlier, Mum had no real memory of being in a foster home or being snatched from there because she was so young at the time and learned the story from her older siblings much later in her life. One thing they often commented on when they met together was that Don was never beaten the way the rest of them were, as he was clearly his father's favourite.

I imagine this favouritism might be because Don was only a toddler when he lost his mother and perhaps his father felt a little guilty, who knows? The children's aunts kept in touch with the children in the years following their sister's death, and they never tried to hide their bitterness towards their brother-in-law, saying that breaking her heart had caused her illness.

I can't possibly imagine the trauma the children endured during these years. The whole of the country was suffering during the depression of course but losing their brother and mother and having a father who was aloof at best and downright cruel at worst must have been extremely dreadful.

The strong bonds I mentioned earlier remained even when the siblings had all moved away and married and, for reasons I fail to understand, they would occasionally meet up together at their father's house on a Sunday afternoon.

It seems strange they would go there, as he had been such a cruel father to them; you would think it would be the last place on earth they would gather.

CHAPTER FOUR

1929

One of Mum's earliest memories was when she was forced to notice the gaping difference between her father's treatment of Don and herself. As they were so close in age, they were perfectly suited as playmates, especially since their sisters and brothers were much older. She told of one sunny Sunday when she was around three and a half and Don was four.

They had been playing a chasing game in the street outside the house with their two friends when their father opened the front door and called them in for lunch. As they reached the door, he steered Don and his friend inside, then pointed Mum through and told her friend to go home for lunch. She felt confused, wondering why her friend wasn't allowed inside.

David often invited important businesspeople in the village to Sunday lunch, and a middle-aged couple were seated at the dining table. The children arrived with shiny faces and clean hands. All the children in the house were on their best behaviour during these lunches; they were required to sit neatly and silently throughout. When lunch was over, the adults headed towards the parlour and the older children headed outside to freedom, but Mum, Don, and his friend were told to come to the parlour.

Mum hated those summonses; it usually meant she and Don were required to entertain the guests by singing or performing a dance or two. The atmosphere in the parlour was stuffy and it was a tense experience for the children, as they had to sit unbearably still for what felt like hours before performing their routine. They were ushered through the door and trooped in obediently.

The parlour contained a much prized, red velvet chaise lounge with a curving arm, a small side table laden with cake and tea, four wooden chairs with straight backs and a walnut writing desk. There were also three small velvet armchairs with buttons in them on which their father and his guests perched. Don's friend was told to sit on a chair while the other two were instructed to begin their little song and dance show.

They did their best impression of Fred Astaire and Ginger Rogers and then Mum was told to sing. She sang the popular Helen Kane song, 'I Wanna Be Loved By You'. Their father liked to show his clever children off to important visitors, the picture of a happy little family. Although they were rarely invited to speak with guests, the children in the house were severely corrected if their language slipped, even slightly, into local slang; they were to speak only 'the Queen's English,' which fitted with their father's vision of the perfect family.

On this occasion, instead of being dismissed immediately from the parlour after the show, Mum was told to sit down in one of the wooden chairs. Father invited Don and his friend to try jumping on the arm of the beautiful chaise lounge and slide down right to the end. The boys didn't have to be asked twice and they were laughing hysterically when they hit the floor after sliding along the smooth velvet. The guests and their father laughed indulgently and encouraged the boys to do it again and again.

Mum sat straight and quiet in her chair, the image of the perfect little princess daughter, trying hard to stop herself from wriggling with impatience as she waited for her turn. Sadly, her father didn't even glance her way while the boys and the guests enjoyed the shenanigans. She knew better than to ask to join in. She realised the rules for Don and the rules for her were different. The 'otherness' she felt that day was to grow even more apparent over time, even though she had no understanding of why it was so.

Don was not subjected to the horrendous beatings his siblings suffered, never bearing his father's wrath on his body, and I wonder how he felt about being singled out in this way. Was he affected later in his life? Did he know why he was spared? I remember my Uncle Don as a quiet man who did well in his business ventures and worked hard.

On trips to Scotland later in my life, I visited him, arriving with a bottle of good Scotch, and we would share a nip or two. During those visits, we would chat about life in general, and he would share a few stories from his time in business. However, we never discussed his childhood. Who knew what trauma lurked behind his lovely eyes; he didn't give much away, and I didn't want to probe.

***

Although the country was beginning to recover from the depths of the Great Depression and sales in the shop were finally improving, David's temper remained ready to explode at any time. The children tried to disappear into the background, hoping to avoid their father's attention. Late one October afternoon, he gave Rab, who was almost ten, such a horrific beating that the boy feared for his life.

When the beating was over, he was thrown, sobbing in pain, into the outside laundry and his father locked the door, ignoring his cries of pain and fear. The bitterly cold evening was closing in, and the concrete laundry would soon become as cold as a morgue.

Margaret, the eldest child at home at the time, was terrified her brother would freeze to death. She paced around the kitchen wringing her hands and wondering what to do. As darkness crept in; she came to a decision. Throwing her warm coat around her, she ran out the door and into the evening gloom. Struggling against the bitter wind, she ran with her heart racing and tears streaming down her face to the blue police box at the corner of the street. She banged her freezing fists on the door frantically, praying the box was still manned. The bobby on duty opened it, a questioning look on his face.

He was obviously preparing to close up for the night, but patiently listened to Margaret's hysterical story as she blurted out her fears for Rab. He gave her the impression that he understood her terror and the predicament at home and promised to investigate, so she trudged home in a slightly calmer state of mind.

The evening crawled by slowly as she waited, with equal parts hope and fear in her heart for someone to come and rescue Rab. She was well aware that the appearance of a rescuer would result in a thrashing from their father. Her anxious wait was in vain, as no police officer arrived that night and it appeared that gentle, timid Margaret had risked so much for nothing.

When the older children arrived home later that night, they took turns to keep watch over Rab all through the long hours, hovering around the laundry door and talking to him. Early the following morning, their father unlocked the door and sat down for breakfast as though nothing had happened. The children were so relieved to see that their brother was alive and was able to take off running like a gold medal winner.

When their father finished his breakfast and readied himself to leave for work, there was a heavy knock on the front door. Agnes answered it to an important looking man dressed in a suit and hat, who flashed his credentials, he was 'the cruelty man.' I'm not sure what department he came from, as there wasn't a Social Services department in those days. For him to arrive so early, I believe the police officer who had heard Margaret's fears must have telephoned his superior with an urgent child welfare report before closing the police box the previous night. Margaret, in her high state of panic, must have managed to convince him that the matter should be investigated with some urgency, as usually the discipline of children was regarded as a family matter.

Well, this visit came too late; Rab was nowhere to be found! David ushered the man into the parlour and muffled voices could be heard for a short time before the door opened and the two men walked to the front door. Before leaving the house, the man shook David's hand; evidently fooled into thinking all was well.

Margaret waited for the inevitable beating, but surprisingly nothing was said and, now late to open the shop, her father rushed out of the door shortly afterwards. Possibly he didn't know who had reported him or perhaps he was so shaken by the early morning visit he forgot to follow through. In either case, his behaviour remained the same and the children were left as defenceless as they had been before the man's visit.

Running away from home became Rab's way of dealing with his father's fury and his escapes led to him being placed many times into institutions such as Dr Barnardo's, a home for wayward and 'bad' boys. When Rab was at home, he often caught his father's eye and suffered many thrashings, but nothing stopped him from running away each time. Hopefully, these types of boys' homes are better places today, but Mum had nothing good to say about them after hearing Rab's stories about the terrible things which went on there.

***

David began arriving home late most nights of the week, which was a relief, but money remained in very short supply and any extra pennies were swallowed up by the growing grocery bills. The children were growing quickly, and there was precious little money to buy them new or even second-hand clothes. Darning, mending, altering clothes and knitting kept them clothed most of the time but a day came when Margaret had to go to school in her old, hand-me-down brownie uniform. It was the only dress she had that wasn't in tatters and she felt dreadfully humiliated. Not having the proper school uniform was all she needed to add to her woes, and she was glad to leave school shortly afterwards.

Around six months after the 'cruelty man' incident, the girls were clearing the lunch dishes away when their father came into the kitchen to tell them he wouldn't be coming home at all the following day, which was a Friday. A ripple of excitement ran through all the children as they heard this news later; on Friday night, they would be free to do as they pleased without their father around. The older children shooed the younger ones out of the kitchen and huddled together to devise a plan. That Friday just happened to be Halloween and they decided to have some fun with their unexpected freedom.

After their father left the next morning, small suitcase in hand, there was a flurry of activity as the little ones were told to invite a friend each to a Halloween party that night. When school finished, the older boys went in search of cheap apples and the largest turnip they could find and scraped the middle out of it. This was a difficult task as turnips are really solid. They were careful to place the mush into a bowl to be used for cooking the next day. When hollowed out, they carved eyes, a nose and a mouth full of teeth into it and placed a candle inside. It looked rather like a skull and was quite terrifying.

In Scotland, turnips grow very large and have been used for hundreds of years at the traditional 'All Hallows Eve,' the precursor to Halloween when people put out the lanterns to frighten away any wandering spirits. They are far more frightening than pumpkins, with their skull-like shapes. The younger children all joined in, making streamers out of old newspaper and carting in the old tin tub from the laundry to fill with water, as instructed. Margaret made a large batch of scones for one of the games they were planning. (She made the most fluffy and delicious ones I have ever tasted.)

That party stood out in Mum's memory, crystal clear, even sixty years later. She remembered it as an amazing and daring adventure, made even more exciting by the fact it was the only party they ever had, and it was all top-secret. They played musical chairs, the Grand Old Duke of York and went 'dooking' for apples, trying not to drown themselves in the process. The highlight of the party was a game of 'treacle scones.'

Thank goodness there was plenty of newspaper on the floor as they laughed and raced to be the first to eat their scone, without getting covered in the sticky treacle. It was a challenging game as the scones were hanging down from the pulley in the kitchen on strings and the treacle dropped down on to their faces and hair. They were forced to chomp furiously at the quivering, unpredictable treats with their hands tied behind them.

After the party finished and their little friends had gone home, everyone worked hard to clean the house as quickly as they could, and scrub themselves clean, ready for bed. The children all fell into bed, totally exhausted, but bubbling with the joy of it all. When their father came home late the next morning, the house appeared as orderly as it should be, and he never suspected a thing. It was to remain the children's delightful secret.

I can only imagine how enchanting that secret party must have been for Mum and the others, even though they didn't have any sweets, balloons or prizes. They had each other, and for once were free to have fun. Parties were rather rare even when I was a child, but I remember how I loved dressing up in a party dress once a year and travelling with Mum by bus to attend the annual children's Christmas party at Dad's workplace. It was marvellous fun taking part in the party games and the amazement of receiving a white cardboard box containing a sandwich, a small packet of crisps, a small bag of sweeties and a gorgeous little fairy cake never faded for me.

After the games were finished Santa arrived amongst much enthusiasm and off-pitch singing, or rather shouting, of the famous 'Jingle Bells' song. He would present each child with a lovely gift, and I would shrug my coat back on and travel home on the bus with Mum, gift carefully clutched in my arms, and my face flushed with excitement.

How the older children organised that rare party emphasises to me the love and care the children had for each other and how the older children tried so hard to give their younger siblings the best life possible, despite their deprivations and punishments. Although she was only around four at the time, Mum clearly remembered every tiny detail of their magical party night and, whenever she spoke of it, her lovely blue eyes would sparkle with delight once again.

CHAPTER FIVE

1930 - 1936

One morning, a few months after their marvellous party, the younger children arrived at the kitchen table for breakfast expecting their normal weak milky tea and toast, or thin watery porridge. To their amazement, they saw a huge pot of steaming, creamy, thick porridge sitting in the centre of the table, along with a large jug of creamy milk.

Their eyes almost popped out of their heads, and they rapidly scoffed their share. A few mornings later, the same thing happened. When they asked where it had come from, Agnes and Margaret shared a conspiratorial glance and said the Good Faery had left it sitting on the window ledge for them.

Over the following month or two, the porridge appeared once or twice a week, occasionally accompanied by a huge pot of thick soup filled with vegetables and meat or a hearty stew with dumplings on top. One evening a tray of baked rice pudding also mysteriously appeared and was rapidly gobbled down. The children were so happy, believing the Good Faery must really love them very much if the scrummy food was any indication. Agnes and Margaret didn't spoil the children's magical dreams.

Around three months after the arrival of the first pot of porridge, there was a flurry of activity as the family packed everything up and moved into a larger flat. The children were not informed as to why they were moving. Although excited by the move, they were also unsettled, as they became aware of Agnes and Margaret holding many whispered conversations in kitchen corners, which abruptly halted when the younger ones appeared.

A week or two following the move into the new house, David ordered the entire family into the parlour early on a Saturday morning. They noticed he was dressed sharply, wearing his best suit and sporting a new fedora. Orders were issued for them to be back in the parlour at 6 pm sharp, scrubbed up and wearing their best clothes. After spending the day wondering what the evening might bring, they nervously washed and polished themselves, and gathered at 6pm sharp as ordered.

When their father came strutting through the parlour door, chest out and smiling, he did not arrive alone. Clutching his arm was a short, stocky woman wearing a long, charcoal dress with matching coat, topped off by a jaunty hat with a flower on it. There was also a flower pinned to her dress; Mum thought she looked ridiculous.

Pacing up and down before the assembled children, their father introduced this woman as his new wife Bessie, who was going to be their new mother. Gripping their father's arm possessively, she turned her pudgy face to them with a smile that never quite reached her eyes.

She said hello in such a broad Scots accent they could hardly understand her. They were instructed to call this woman 'mother' and ordered to make her welcome. Orders were also issued to obey her implicitly from now on and to make room for her two children, who were due to arrive the following day.

Finally excused, the children filed out into the hallway with slumped shoulders and bowed heads. The older ones exchanged knowing, worried glances before going about their usual chores; they were not impressed at all by their new 'mother.' They had suspected their father was courting a woman and that she was the one who had provided the lovely meals. Although they had dubbed her 'The Good Faery' for the young ones, they seriously questioned whether she would prove to be the caring stepmother they needed.

The next day, just before Sunday lunch, two people arrived, suitcases in hand. The young man introduced himself as Alex, and the pretty young woman with him as Alice. The new house was now filled to bursting point and within days the older children were arguing, especially the three older girls. Agnes and Margaret were sharing their bedroom with Alice and there were many screaming matches regarding missing stockings or the mess on the dressing table. Bessie quickly took control of the household and promptly started bossing the children around.

To add to the tension, Agnes and Margaret struggled to accept Bessie as their stepmother. They had, after all, taken care of the house and the younger children since their mother had become ill four years earlier. Within a few weeks of Bessie's arrival, David became fed up with his new wife's complaints about the children and flew into a frenzy. He ordered Agnes, Margaret and Jimmy, along with Bessie's two kids, out of the house for good. This left only the three youngest, Mum, Don, and Rab at home, in between Rab's stints in the boys' home.

After being thrown out of the house, Jimmy, Agnes, and Margaret were abandoned, left to make new lives for themselves. Davey had already left home, having stowed away on a ship. He then joined the Merchant Navy as a cook and at the end of the war, settled in Canada for a while. There are conflicting stories about what he did there, he either joined the 'Mounties' or opened a grocery store which failed because he kept giving credit to the needy. He then returned to Edinburgh and worked in some of Edinburgh's top hotels as a cook, including the R & B hotel which was very famous in those days.

He was a bit of a rascal though, and his antics often led to him being sacked for mischievous incidents. One example was when he was caught sneaking into the dumb waiter to get up to the maids' quarters.

Jimmy became a bottle washer in a hotel and eventually worked his way up to become a waiter. Over time, he was promoted to head waiter at the Café Royal; a very expensive, classy restaurant which was frequented by Edinburgh's elite.

Agnes and Margaret were only seventeen and fifteen when they were thrown out of the house. They were lucky to know someone who found them work in the City Hospital in

Edinburgh. The matron of the hospital took them under her wing and made sure they had bed and board in the nurses home. Although their accommodation was basic, bare and usually cold, they worked hard and were able to relax at the end of the day, safe from their father, and this change alone made it wonderful. Within a short time, Agnes moved on from there into service in a well to do household.

Margaret also went into service, but she returned home a few times over the next couple of years when she was between tenures, only to be thrown out again within a week or two.

After Alex and Alice were thrown out, Mum didn't see them for a long time and didn't know what had happened to them. However, they did visit their mother once or twice during the following years but remained as shadows to Mum.

With her sisters and older brothers gone, Mum and Don felt the house was very empty, sad, and silent. Bessie had replaced Agnes as female head of the house, but she was quite distant from them unless she required a task done. They especially missed Margaret's gentle loving care.

They had been given strict orders from their father never to contact their older siblings. *"Furthermore,"* he demanded, *"if you accidently bump into any of them, you must ignore them entirely."* This order was terribly hard for the children,

The children soon learned Bessie was not the Good Faery of their dreams but was a stepmother who was detached and disinterested in them. She was a great cook, making good wholesome meals for the family but was not given to providing the kind of care a young child needs. She allocated daily chores to the children; particularly Mum, but apart from giving orders, she basically ignored the children unless they failed to carry out the chores as directed or dared to disobey her. To their dismay, they quickly discovered that she would tell their father if they didn't follow her orders implicitly; and there would be hell to pay.

Mum's chores were mostly in the kitchen. Although she was accustomed to completing many kitchen chores, she now hated them because Bessie was an extremely messy cook. She seemed to use every dish in the house when cooking or baking and carelessly scattered flour and sugar everywhere. Mum's daily chores were to set and clear the table, lay out her father's tea tray, wash the dishes and sweep the kitchen floor.

***

Both Don and Mum were packed off to school together in September, although Mum was not yet five. She found school overwhelming and was very anxious when she arrived through the gates with Don. Noisy children were running around the tarmac playground, screeching and chasing each other. It was frightening. She pressed close to her brother for protection, and within minutes, a stern-looking woman appeared in the huge doorway and rang a big brass bell very loudly.

When the children quietened down and followed her instructions to gather, she proceeded to call out names one by one, and indicate where that child should stand. The swarm magically formed into lines. When Mum's name was called, she reluctantly let go of Don's shirt and stood where indicated, knees shaking. Don was called next and sent to a different line and off they marched into separate classrooms.

Being extremely shy, Mum would never ask her strict teacher for help when she was confused and, with over forty pupils to wrestle into submission, the exhausted woman had no time to notice the quiet ones who merged into the background. Struggling to grasp the early concepts of reading and writing, Mum learned to be as quiet as a mouse, hoping to become invisible.

In many ways the classroom was an environment of fear for her, not so different to home. It was the start of her difficult passage through formal education, a journey which continued to be challenging throughout her entire school years.

Within a few months of starting school, both Don and Mum became seriously ill with a high fever and a bright red rash developed all over their bodies. They were diagnosed with Scarlet Fever and rushed to hospital by ambulance. In the pre-penicillin days, Scarlet Fever was a severe, life-threatening illness and they were hospitalised for over a month.

Thankfully they were together in the children's ward and as they slowly recovered, they kept each other amused with tricks and games, and became closer than ever. Their father visited every Sunday afternoon, bringing a comic or fruit for Don before sitting beside his bed for most of the hour. After visiting his son, he would spend a few cursory moments with Mum before leaving.

Apart from the familiar feeling of being rejected, Mum only remembers one awful thing about that time: head lice! One night when the nurses came to tidy the bed for lights out, they discovered a louse crawling on her pillow and looked over the bed at each other in horror: those horrible blood sucking parasites can spread like wildfire. They knew if the infection spread to any of the other children, they would both be disciplined by Matron for having a dirty ward.

One of the nurses spirited Mum away into the cold bathroom, while the other changed the linens and disinfected the mattress. Mum's hair was washed and towel dried, and the nurse doused her head with kerosene. She wrapped brown paper and linen around it. As she climbed back into bed, Mum's head felt as if it was on fire, and she begged the nurse to wash it off. She was told that if it was washed off before morning, they would have to shave her hair off.

She tried hard to be good but sobbed into her pillow all night as the horrible stuff stung her scalp. When her hair was finally washed early the following morning, she cried with relief but unfortunately the relief was short lived. The dreaded beasts came back within days and her lovely thick hair was shaved anyway. Dismayed, she examined herself in the bathroom mirror; only to see a young boy with a crew cut peering back at her.

On her return to school, Mum found her month away had left her even further behind the other children. She knew she looked rather weird and was terribly embarrassed about her hair and wanted to crawl into the woodwork to hide. Overall, it was a difficult return to her schooling.

She continued to suffer from ill health throughout her school years and her absences added to her struggles to understand Arithmetic and English. I now believe she may have suffered from dyslexia and, as I grew older, I came to understand she was a very bright, intelligent woman.

I say this now despite being aware of her dreadful spelling and grammar, not to mention her apparent lack of general knowledge. I'm ashamed to remember my attitude to her poorly written notes to my teachers which often embarrassed me, I was always good at English, and these notes often made me cringe.

***

The family moved house a number of times over the next two years, without explanation, although it was possibly because their father was sent to manage different stores in villages across the East Coast of the country. Their final move, was to the vast, bustling, capital city of Edinburgh. Their new flat was on the ground floor of a stone tenement in Easter Road with a door opening directly onto the busy street.

It was all so far removed from the peaceful villages where they had lived before. Although they were excited by the new experience of the bustling city, the children found it to be very dark and smoky, with grey buildings surrounding them. The Clean Air Act had yet to be legislated; it didn't happen until the mid-1950's and Edinburgh deserved its old nickname of 'Auld Reekie' or 'Old Smoky.'

It described the city's miasma of dark smelly pollution which emanated from all the houses and tenements which relied on coal fires for heating and cooking. Every chimney belched black smoke into the air and a clear blue sky was rarely on show. The stone walls of every store and tenement were grimed black with soot and, when people blew their noses, their handkerchiefs were stained black. Nevertheless, their father was happy to have a much larger store to manage, with a larger salary to boot, and his mood even improved a little.

Life settled into a never-ending round of chores for Mum. By the time she was ten, her responsibilities were: sweeping and washing the kitchen floor, setting and clearing the table, washing and drying the evening dishes, polishing the brass and silver, starching her father's collars, and ironing. On Sunday nights, she was also required to blacken the kitchen range and, worst of all, darn her father's socks and her own woollen stockings and knickers. Darning is a highly skilled way to mend holes in woollen items by weaving a smooth patch with a needle and wool. All her tasks had to be completed perfectly but she especially dreaded the darning. If her father felt even one tiny bump in her work, he would throw it at her with a sneer, slap her face and make her unpick and redo it perfectly.

She learned from a very early age to keep quiet, do her work flawlessly and keep out of the way as much as possible. Remembering those days, she often said she felt like a dummy or a zombie, going to school, doing her work and silently tiptoeing around the house.

In her writing, Mum describes one Sunday night in particular. The evening had unfolded in the normal manner and after supper she was sitting in the kitchen, enjoying the last heat from the range and doing the weekly darning under the light of the standard lamp. Afterwards, she took her weekly bath and crawled thankfully into bed, falling instantly into a deep, well-deserved sleep.

She was wakened sometime later by a sharp blow to the head and found herself being dragged out of bed by her hair.

Staggering to stand up, she became aware her father was right in front of her, shouting at her to follow him into the kitchen at once! The whole house was in darkness; it seemed to be the wee hours of the morning. Shaking with fear, she scurried through the hallway and into the freezing kitchen where her father was standing by the lamp, his eyes burning with rage.

She came to stand, quaking, before him and he shoved a pair of her navy school knickers in her face. His finger was pushed inside the knickers and was poking through a hole she hadn't noticed earlier. He hit her hard around the head again while roaring at her; his spittle flying into the air, telling her to darn them properly before going back to bed.

After he left the room, she sat by the lamp again and bent to her task, but it was difficult to see through the tears pouring from her eyes. Trembling with shock and the freezing cold, she struggled to calm herself and complete the work. Almost numb with cold, she crawled into bed afterwards and fell into a troubled sleep.

When reading Mum's descriptions of this cruelty and other similar incidents, I find myself wondering for the millionth time … why? Why did her father feel the need to go through all the darning, obviously looking for imperfections, so he could release his rage on his daughter? It was the same thing he had done to her older sisters, wiping across the furniture, checking for dust. I can't imagine living in perpetual fear the way these children did.

CHAPTER SIX

1936

It was a wonderful surprise when Mum discovered her sister Margaret was living somewhere close by. A few weeks earlier, Mum had noticed her in the distance as she stepped off a bus near the corner of Easter Road and Lorne Street. Sprinting to the corner, she peered down Lorne Street, but she had disappeared.

Doggedly, she asked around the girls at school until eventually she discovered that Margaret was boarding with the aunt of one of her own classmates. Such good news. She wrote the address down and folded it up in her sweaty hand.

When her father and Bessie were out of the house the following evening, she told Don the amazing news and, barely containing their delight, they ran to the address. After knocking on the door, they hopped from foot to foot, and waited impatiently. Margaret answered the door and their sister's eyes grew round with surprise to see them on the doorstep.

Reaching out, she swiftly pulled them together into a brisk hug and hustled them into the house; they had to be careful not to be seen by any tattle tales. All three were laughing and crying at the same time as Margaret ushered them into a cosy living room.

They stayed there for more than an hour, talking eagerly through mouths filled with tea and cake, sharing news about their lives. Mum was especially excited to tell Margaret about the dancing lessons she had begun attending in the local hall. Her sister was thrilled for her, knowing how much she loved to dance.

Margaret said she had recently started work as a waitress in the R & B hotel, a real step up from her last job serving meals in a pub in Leith. Bubbling and tripping over her words, she revealed her most thrilling news: she was being courted by a lovely young man by the name of David McIntosh. She had caught his eye while she was serving in the pub where his cricket team gathered after their Saturday game, and it didn't take long for him to pluck up enough courage to ask her out.

The two rebellious children knew they would be in the deepest trouble if they were caught there, but thankfully it was summer, and they were allowed to stay outside until 9.00 pm. Seeing their beloved sister so well and happy made their steps light as they made their way home, whispering their thoughts about Margaret's news of a beau.

A few weeks after this visit, Mum came barrelling out of the local corner shop one Saturday morning, hands filled with string bags of shopping and crashed right into her sister. They laughingly said that this was the most they had seen each other for years. They quickly shared a little news before Mum said goodbye and turned for home, just as Margaret put out a hand to stop her. *"I have a great idea"* she said, *"David and I are going out tonight to see a variety show in the Theatre Royal, would you like to come with us"?*

Well, you wouldn't have to ask Mum twice, *"Oh yes please"* she squealed, twirling around and around. However, she soon sobered, knowing she would have to see Bessie to gain permission and asked Margaret to wait at home for her until late afternoon before taking off at a run.

Mad with delight, she darted straight home, the shopping bags jiggling in her hands. She dashed into the kitchen and, without thinking of the consequences of having spoken to her sister, she breathlessly asked Bessie if she could go. Her stepmother, annoyed at having her quiet cup of tea interrupted, half listened to her request and sent her to ask her father. Mum, still irrational in her happiness, rushed to the shop and found her father behind the counter, serving a customer. Red-faced with eagerness, she stood impatiently, hugging herself to contain her news, until the customer left. As soon as the doorbell jangled behind the customer, she foolishly blurted out her request.

Her father fixed her with an icy look, saying *"Well, of course not,"* snapping her temporarily to her senses! Dejected, she left the store when he turned away, dismissing her coldly. The temptation of spending time with Margaret and attending the theatre was strong; strong enough to force her to devise a scheme. At eleven years old she was shrewd enough to come up with a workable plan which she put into action as soon as she was home.

She worked extra hard to complete her chores quickly and to perfection. As soon as she finished, she mentioned casually to Bessie that she was spending the day at her friend's house where she had been invited for supper. Promising to be home by her 10.00pm weekend curfew, she floated out of the front door and ran to meet Margaret at her house as arranged.

Mum could hardly contain her joy as she walked with Margaret and David to the bus stop for the short ride to the theatre district. Mum immediately warmed to David who was quite tall and spoke quietly in a lilting highlander accent. He impressed her with his gentlemanly ways. She was happy to see her gentle sister on the arm of such a fine young man.

They enjoyed a bite of supper in a café before the performance, with soup and little sandwiches, followed by ice cream with a little triangular wafer on top. The show was an absolute dream, fulfilling Mum's every fantasy of how exciting theatre might be. She felt so alive and happy.

At the end of the show, she couldn't help but skip like a delighted child on the way to the bus stop, and thanked David as he boarded his own bus home. The sisters giggled as they said goodnight after leaving their bus and turned in different directions to head home. Mum couldn't help singing her favourite song from the show and practicing a few dance steps she had seen as she pranced down the street. She was keen to remember the new moves so she could show them to her dance teacher.

Still in another world, she reached the door and turned the handle, only to find the door wouldn't budge. She was puzzled.

Why was it locked she thought? Margaret had told her it was 9.45 when they parted just a minute ago, so she was well within her deadline. The door was always left unlocked until everyone was home at night, curfews being strictly imposed.

Frowning in confusion, she grasped the brass bell handle which she kept gleaming and pulled. Within seconds she let out a scream when, with one swift move, the door opened, and she was pulled into the hallway by her hair. It was her father who held her hair as he hit her again and again across the head and dragged her by her arm into her bedroom.

She could feel that she was wetting herself but was powerless to stop the urine flowing down her legs. When he had forced her into the bedroom, her father pushed her down onto the bed and punched her all over her body until she passed out.

Her next memory was of stirring just enough to hear Margaret and her father shouting in the hallway. She heard her sister screaming in pain before she blacked out again. When she awoke the second time, she found that she couldn't move her body and was only able to see a little through her half-closed eyes.

Peering painfully into the light, she saw Margaret crouching on the floor next to her bed, sobbing. She was dabbing a cold, damp cloth on Mum's face, which felt good, but then she passed out again.

When she became aware for the third time, she could move a little and could see, although not clearly. The first thing she noticed was that there was blood and shit smeared all over the wall next to her bed, the smell was overpowering.

Margaret was scrubbing furiously at the mess and when she finished, she stood Mum up and changed the sheets before lying down beside her. They lay together side by side, just looking at each other until Mum fell into a deep sleep. When she woke up in the early hours of the morning, she was bereft to see the empty space in the bed where her sister had lain. She was alone again.

When Mum occasionally spoke to my siblings and I about the beatings she received from her father; she always had a hard time explaining them. Her mouth would close into a thin line before she unclamped her lips again. She told us she honestly thought she was going to die that time. Then she would change the subject abruptly.

Personally, I think it was a mercy she passed out when she did and was unaware of the damage being inflicted on her. Nevertheless, in her writing it is obvious that remembering this vicious beating caused her a great deal of distress, as her pen has underlined the words *"I thought I was going to die"* a number of times, scoring the page through until it feels bumpy, like braille, underneath.

My heart aches when I read Mum's words as she tries to describe this thumping. They say at times of extreme fear, a person's bowels can turn to water and now I understand how true the saying is. In writing about this, I had to read her words many times, and every reading troubled me deeply once again. I was aching for this eleven-year-old girl, my mother, as she hurls her words onto the page, fifty years after suffering such brutality at the hands of the man who should have been her protector.

Mum later learned of how Margaret had come to her rescue. She had waited at the bus stop on the corner of Easter Road to watch her little sister skip safely home. Seeing Mum reach the door, she was about to turn towards home herself when she heard the blood-curdling scream as Mum was dragged inside. Margaret rushed down the street and raced right through the open front door, straight into Mum's bedroom where she could hear her father shouting. Quickly taking in the scene, she shouted at her father to stop, clawing at him uselessly to pull him away from Mum.

It took what seemed like hours for him to straighten up, and when he did, he turned his wild eyes on Margaret. He hit her across the face, and she ran back into the hall where, fortunately for her, she received only a few slaps before he came out of his insane rage. He pushed her aside and headed down the hall into his own bedroom, slamming the door behind him.

Don also told Mum how her scheme had been uncovered. On the Saturday evening, two business associates of their father's had stopped by with their wives in tow. Don was promptly dispatched to fetch Mum from her friend's house as she was needed to help serve tea and clean up. Of course, when Don asked for Mum at her friend's house, her deception was discovered.

CHAPTER SEVEN

1937

Around six months after this terrible night, when Mum was twelve years old, she became seriously ill. She had recently suffered from a dreadful throat infection and a constant fever which kept her confined to bed for weeks. When she had recovered sufficiently, she was sent back to school although she still felt weak and shaky.

In any case, within a few days of her return, she was sent home because she had been crying all day. She had excruciating pains in her legs and feet and the high fever had returned. She hobbled back to the house; a walk that took well over an hour instead of the usual fifteen minutes, because she had to keep stopping to rest. When she arrived home and limped through the kitchen door, Bessie sighed and sent her back to bed.

Bringing a glass of water and some aspirin to her, Bessie saw that she was asleep but noticed the blankets were pushed right down to the bottom of the bed, leaving Mum cold. Bessie drew the blankets up, but as soon as they touched her legs, Mum screamed out in dreadful pain.

Even a light sheet was enough to start the screaming off again and Bessie took a closer look. On inspection, she noticed Mum's legs were red and swollen and became worried. The doctor was called to examine her but said he couldn't find anything wrong. *"Just a fever,"* was his diagnosis and he prescribed bed rest and aspirin.

Mum lay in agonising pain until two days later when a neighbour stopped by for a cup of tea and a gossip and asked how the sick child was. On hearing she was still unwell; she popped her head into the bedroom and attempted to pull the blankets over her. This brought renewed screams of agony, and the kindly woman felt her forehead to test her temperature. *"Good grief, this bairn is burning up"* she exclaimed and, on hearing that a doctor had already been to see her, she suggested calling her own doctor to come.

Mum was immediately declared to be critically ill with rheumatic fever, and she was whisked away in an ambulance. Rheumatic fever was often fatal in the days before antibiotics were available, and left untreated, causes severe heart damage. This heart damage is known as Rheumatic Heart Disease (RHD). Mum was one of the lucky children who survived although she did spend over three months in hospital and was left with lifelong damage to her heart.

While in hospital, she became the darling of the nurses and female patients in her ward. When she had recovered enough to get around in a wheelchair, she would spin across the ward from bed to bed, chatting with the ladies and entertaining them with the latest songs. The nurses were happy to let her help tidy the lockers and arrange flowers before Matron's inspection rounds. Her presence cheered everyone up.

Over her months in hospital, Don was her only visitor. He popped in faithfully every Saturday afternoon when he finished his shift at the nearby cinema, bringing her a small gift every time: strawberries, a comic or even some sweeties which he bought with his small wage. Seeing him was the highlight of Mum's week; she eagerly waited for his visits and was sad when he left, knowing she would have to wait seven whole days before he came to see her again.

Sometimes people who had come to visit other patients during visiting hours would stop to chat with her for a while when they noticed she was alone. Neither Bessie nor her father came and, as the older children no longer lived at home, they didn't know she was in hospital.

Over time, Mum became strong enough to leave the wheelchair and take a few shaky steps. As she had sustained severe damage to her heart during the early days of her illness, it had taken all the medical treatment the doctors had at their disposal to save her life. The excruciating inflammation, coupled with the months of bed rest, had weakened the muscles in her legs, and she started the painful task of learning to walk again.

After months in hospital, a letter was sent to her father saying that Mum was ready to be discharged. Bessie was despatched to collect her. Before Mum was allowed to leave, the doctor had a long discussion with Bessie describing the seriousness of her heart condition and giving precise instructions as to what the child should and shouldn't be doing. It was made clear that she should not exert herself by walking too far, climbing hills or stairs or lifting anything heavy. He said it would take time for her to regain her strength and, as she was extremely underweight, build her back up again to an acceptable level.

When they emerged from the building which had been Mum's haven for the past few months, they headed for the bus stop. Walking was difficult as Mum's legs were weak, and she moved slowly, trailing her feet behind her a little. Despite her weird gait, she was proud of the hard work she had put in to learn to walk again. Although happy to be breathing the fresh air, she turned and sent a last sad glance to the hospital where she had been safe.

Walking slowly into the dark hallway of the house, the ever-present mantle of fear and trepidation surrounded her again. Thankfully her father was not at home and, exhausted from the trip home, she fell straight into bed. She was spared from seeing her father for the next few days and spent her time sleeping, resting or playing cards with Don after he arrived home from school.

On the first Sunday afternoon at home, Bessie came into the bedroom where she was resting and said, *"Git away ben to your faither and show him how you can walk the noo."* There was nothing else for it, so with head held high to cover her nervousness, she knocked on the parlour door and tentatively entered when invited. Closing the door behind her, she bravely said, *"See father, I can walk again"'* and walked slowly across the carpet towards the table where he was seated.

He looked up from his newspaper, his glance aloof as usual, and watched on dispassionately as she made her halting way towards him.

She tried so hard to make her feet keep up with her legs but was frustrated that, despite her best efforts, they still trailed behind her. *"Ha, do you call that walking?"* he sneered, before flicking the newspaper out and turning the page. He went back to his reading, effectively dismissing her. Although she was used to his cruelty by now and was past crying, she slowly backed out of the parlour without saying another word and continued her hollow existence.

Only a few days after showing her father she could walk again; she was instructed to resume all the chores which had been her responsibility before her illness. A few weeks later, in addition to her household chores, she was also ordered to assist her father in the shop every Saturday morning. When she was in the shop, he would send her up the two flights of stairs to the stockroom to collect a particular size or style of shoe for a customer.

The climb was arduous, as she could only clamber up each step, gripping the handrail and catching her breath every few minutes. With the correct shoes clutched under her arm, she would struggle back down the stairs. No matter how difficult it was, she complied; after all, it was impossible to say no to her father.

When talking about her battle with rheumatic fever, Mum would often say being forced to do her chores and to work on Saturday mornings, although very difficult for her at the time, may have helped her rebuild her strength. The illness leaves a sufferer with a damaged heart, and they are often unable to enjoy a full life. Thankfully, the illness is almost unknown in our modern, affluent society and can be treated with antibiotics before devastating heart damage occurs.

Mum often spoke fondly of a girl she met while in hospital and who also suffered from the same illness. Claire was fourteen and had already been in hospital for a month when Mum arrived. They instantly became friends and generally had as much fun as possible, playing board or card games together. When Claire was able to walk a little, she was discharged and her granny, whom she lived with, collected her in a wheelchair. Before Claire left the ward, she and Mum promised to remain friends forever and write to each other regularly.

When Mum was older and working in the city, she would occasionally meet Claire and her granny for lunch, but sadly her pale friend remained frail, and wheelchair bound. Mum received a letter one morning from Claire's granny, bearing the sad news that her granddaughter had died of heart failure. She was only seventeen.

Mum believed her heart had failed because her grandmother had mollycoddled her, caring for her a bit too much. I'm not sure her theory was true, but I believe this philosophy tells volumes about Mum's character. When she went on to raise three children, she would often say, *"Just pull your socks up and get on with it."* or *"There's no point crying over spilt milk,"* she was certainly not about to mollycoddle us. Although her love was unconditional, it was also tough.

Having said that, she loved us deeply and cared for us to the very best of her ability. Sometimes it took all her strength and tenacity to do so. We all have fond memories of the times we were ill as children. We all suffered from the many nasty illnesses that were rife in those days including measles, chicken pox, whooping cough, mumps, bronchitis and the flu. At those times, she would make up a comfortable bed for us on the sofa, close to the warm fire, and cook us her famous scrambled eggs with cheese. Sometimes she also bought us a huge treat, such as Lucozade or Ribena, so I shouldn't be too harsh on her efforts to build resilient children.

Although Mum eventually became strong enough to walk properly again, her badly damaged heart caused her to be plagued by illness and frustrating fainting spells for the rest of her life. We children remember the many times we would arrive home from school, only to find her passed out cold on the kitchen floor. There were also times when we found her leaning over the kitchen sink, running cold water over her wrists in a desperate effort to revive herself after fainting.

Whichever unlucky kid arrived home from school first, only to see her lying on the floor, would sigh dramatically in frustration and begin the 'recovery' procedure. We began by loosening her collar, then slapping her hands, wrists and cheeks and calling "Mum, Mum" until she opened her eyes and gulped a giant breath. When she was able to crawl over to a chair, we would settle her with a glass of water and quickly scarper off to play. I know this sounds terribly uncaring, but we were so used to her 'spells', they were a large part of the landscape of our childhood and were more annoying to us than frightening.

Mum's love for us was genuine and unconditional. She showed it in many different ways, but what I remember from childhood most keenly are her last words at night. Regardless of how the day had unfolded, she would tuck us in, or pop her head around the door as we grew older, and leave us with the words, *"Always remember I love you!"* We may have been punished harshly during the day for disobedience or for lying to her... a huge no-no, but the day would always end this way.

Naturally, we would sometimes think 'sure you do' as our bums may have still been smarting or our ears ringing from being shouted at, but she made such an effort to make sure we all knew we were loved. I will always be thankful to her for the security those words gave me, even though I didn't fully appreciate their importance at the time.

***

Although Mum knew her father favoured Don above her, nothing could have prepared her for the words which came out of her brother's mouth one sunny Saturday afternoon. They had been playing a game of rounders - a game not unlike baseball - with some friends in the local park when, in typical sibling fashion, they started arguing ferociously about a rule in the game.

They continued to be furious with each other as they stomped home, Don leading the way. In a final, desperate, ploy to ensure his victory, he drew upon some newfound knowledge. He turned to face her and shouted, "And anyway, you're not even my sister!" Mum stopped, mouth open, for a second before loudly countering with the typical kid response; "Are too" … to which Don retorted "Are not" etc …

The to-ing and fro-ing continued, in the age-old way of siblings, until Don completely lost his temper, and yelled … "You can't be my sister because babies take nine months to come out and I'm only eight months older than you … so there!"

With those final poisonous words thrown carelessly but irretrievably into the air, he rushed off ahead of her and slammed into the house. "What?" … Mum stood rooted to the spot, stunned into silence, mouth open. Eventually she stirred herself and tiptoed into the house, scorching tears racing down her face and an unbearable pain in her heart. After cleaning herself up, she went about her usual kitchen chores in a perplexed daze, disoriented by her brother's angry words.

All throughout the long night, she tossed and turned in her bed, confused by his words and unable to sleep, her bewilderment leaving her with more questions than answers. She had relied on her siblings for safety and affection, especially Don, because they were the only two children left at home after the others were thrown out. What if she didn't belong? As the sleepless night dragged on, her pain developed into a great anger.

The following morning, unable to contain the fury which had been building through the night for a moment more, she took the unthinkable step of knocking on her father's bedroom door. Unbelievably, she didn't wait for his reply before barging in, only stopping short and freezing in the open doorway when she saw her father and Bessie sitting up in bed enjoying their Sunday morning newspapers as usual.

The enormity of her blunder immobilised her for a second when she saw her father was about to begin screaming at her. Her heart in her mouth and a sinking feeling in her stomach, she considered blurting an apology and running back out of the door before his rage exploded.

Yet, such was the level of her anger and pain, she couldn't stop herself from crying out … "Don keeps saying that I'm not his sister, but I am so, aren't I?" Her father surveyed her for a few heart stopping minutes before, quite calmly and clearly, he shattered her hopes by coolly saying… "As a matter of fact, you are not, you were adopted when you were six weeks old." The cruel words cut straight and true, right into her heart! She felt as though a knife had been plunged into it, and the room appeared to darken around her, leaving her unable to move for a beat. She was shaken from her stupor by her father bellowing for her to "Get out!"

Despite feeling vomit rise in her throat, she turned and soundlessly slunk from the room, closing the door silently behind her. Standing outside the bedroom door, she experienced the sensation of all the air and light being sucked out of her body, leaving only a vacuum where there had been feelings and emotions.

She now understood why she had always felt different from her brother, aside from the obvious fact he was his father's favourite. She now believed she was not part of the Bell family at all; she didn't belong with any of them, including her beloved sister Margaret. It was as though she continued to live in the house but was separated from everyone by a veil. She was an orphan, truly alone in the world.

It became harder after this heartbreaking revelation for her to relate to any of the family, especially since she hardly saw the older ones anymore. Apart from being forbidden to see them, they were much older than she and Don, and had families and lives of their own. Her loneliness caused her to retreat into her shell whenever she was inside the house, and to exist only in an emotionless, almost robotic state.

CHAPTER EIGHT

1937-1938

Not long after being told she was adopted at six weeks of age, Bessie called Mum into the kitchen one Sunday morning. This was surprising, as Bessie usually stayed in bed with father until eleven on Sundays. Wondering if she was in trouble, Mum arrived to see Bessie sitting at the table and reading the morning newspapers with a cup of tea in her hand.

Looking up from her newspaper, Bessie said, '*Get away ben the bedroom, your faither wants to see you.*' With her heart hammering thunderously in her chest, Mum dragged herself to the bedroom door and knocked, all the while racking her brains for anything she had done to be sent there. It was quite obvious to her that she was in trouble.

When her father called for her to come in, she crept into the room and stood close to the open door, eyes downcast. After a moment, she stole a glance towards him and saw him sitting up in bed, looking at her appraisingly. He told her to close the door and come closer to the bed, and she inched forward with shaking knees.

In a low voice, most unlike the shouting she was expecting to hear, he told her to take her shoes off. Naturally, she obeyed, her trembling hands making it hard to get the laces undone, and looked up at him, perplexed. In the same low, kindly sounding voice, he told her to take her dress off and to climb up into the bed beside him.

Dazed and trembling, she hesitated, as she tried to figure out what was going on; what on earth did this mean? After a few moments which felt like a lifetime, she realised there was no choice but to obey; disobedience was never an option. She pulled her dress over her head and climbed up into the bed wearing only her vest and bloomers.

As she shivered next to him, she was astonished to hear him speaking quietly and gently, saying strange things to her in a tender voice. He turned to her and began to caress her thin childish body; down her arms, across her chest, and sliding down to rub her stomach. Moving down from there, he stroked her in places she knew were shameful to touch.

As all this was happening to her, she found herself becoming completely numb, her fear vanished along with all other feelings; and she felt herself drift out of her body. She looked on from somewhere above and realised her body was still in the bed with her father's hands on her. These hands had never touched her in the past, other than to deliver blows, and she merely looked on dispassionately. He continued to do what he wanted with the lifeless, empty shell, that lay there.

When it was over, he sent her a disgusted, withering look and told her to get dressed and leave. She scurried out of the bed to obey, scooping up her dress, and pulling it over her head, before grabbing her shoes and rushing through the door.

She left the bedroom a very different person; any childhood innocence savagely torn away forever. Desperate for the safety of her own bedroom, she fell in through the door and saw herself in the wall mirror. Drawing closer, she was shocked to see only her own reflection: how could it be that she looked exactly the same as when she had brushed her hair early that morning? She felt so different now; somehow empty and detached, but at the same time filled to overflowing with guilt.

It never occurred to her to go to anyone for help. She couldn't tell Bessie who, after all, had sent her in to the bedroom in the first place and who had never come to her rescue during father's rages. No, Bessie was not to be trusted; at all, she always trotted straight to father with tales of Mum's misdemeanours. There was no one she could go to.

Mum was often sent to her father's bed over the next two years or so. The deep feelings of shame and humiliation she suffered ensured the abuse remained locked inside her, a terrible secret, for over fifty years. When I think about the repulsive abuse Mum endured, I wonder, not for the first time, whether Bessie had any idea what was going on during those mornings?

As I absorb Mum's words as she attempted to describe this abuse, it is clear to me she was unable to explain the horror inflicted on her. I am sure she didn't have the words to express it. She did, however, write that these mornings had *"put her past sex*," adding how she didn't like any part of her body to be touched.

It is impossible for me to imagine the trauma she bore as a result of this new type of cruelty, and I marvel, once again, at her extraordinary resilience. I'm certain she must have waited fearfully for each Sunday to come around, the weekdays speeding by far too quickly. She prayed each week she would be spared.

Up until this time, Mum disliked and feared her father, but now she absolutely hated him with a deep and seething anger! Research has now revealed the psychological trauma caused by incest, leading me into a better understanding of why I sensed something, or someone unknown, deep inside my Mum, and beyond my reach.

***

When Mum was fifteen, she began to menstruate. She was working by that time and her period started at work. Knowing nothing about periods, she was terrified to find herself bleeding when she went to the toilet. She travelled home on the bus after work with wads of toilet paper stuck inside her knickers, petrified in case she was bleeding to death.

She was so afraid that as soon as she entered the house, she went straight to the kitchen and told Bessie something was wrong. When she explained she was bleeding 'down there,' Bessie, calmly said *"Och you're just like the coos in the fields."* She gave her some clean rags, a length of elastic and two large safety pins, and showed her how to make pads. She told her to attach the pads to the elastic to hold the blood and to make sure to soak them every night. They were all to be boiled together after her periods were over, ready for the next month.

What a hassle, she thought, hardly able to believe what she was hearing. She was relieved to realise that at least she wasn't dying but wasn't impressed to learn it would happen every month from now on.

It was around the time of her first period that the summonses to her father's bedroom stopped. If it was the arrival of her messy, horrible and painful periods which stopped him, I'm sure she would have thought the pain and trouble were a small price to pay for her rescue. One wonders if the abuse stopped because he knew he could now get her pregnant.

That Mum wasn't the only girl in the family to be sexually abused by their father seems certain. While she was visiting Scotland on holiday, she told us, she had attempted to discuss the incest she had suffered with Margaret; Agnes having passed away by that time. They were both worldly-wise grandmothers, and Mum had become more tormented by her memories as she aged. She wanted to unburden her secret and talk it over with her beloved sister.

As soon as she raised the subject, all the colour drained from Margaret's face and, in a furious voice, she spat out, *"Och, he was such a filthy old man."* She immediately turned away from Mum and hurriedly bustled off to do something, refusing to speak of it any further. Her daughters, my dear cousins, Anne and Joan, told me their mother had never spoken about any sexual abuse with them. Although, over the years, they surmised from small clues here and there that she did not escape his abuse either.

I remember that our mums never left us alone with their father when we would occasionally go there for a fleeting visit, usually with my Auntie Margaret and Joan. The mums always seemed on edge, nervously glancing everywhere and speaking mostly with Bessie. My memories of the house are of a dark hallway, a plush parlour and the sound of the golden carriage clock slowly ticking away the tension-filled minutes until we could leave. Joan shares similar memories and I often wonder why we went there.

As far as I'm aware, Mum's older sister, Agnes, never revealed whether or not she had suffered any sexual abuse as a child. Sadly, though, her early adult life appears to have been littered with broken and sometimes abusive relationships. Apparently, she desperately craved the attention of men, and this kind of behaviour is often seen in women who have suffered child sexual abuse.

I remember her as a beautiful, but rather stern, woman who spoke with a posh voice and wore nice clothes. She lived in a big fancy house and took holidays in a beautiful guesthouse by the beach in the village of Aberdour where there was a summerhouse, tea and cakes. Joan and I loved to visit her there, travelling by steam train with our Mums, so thrilled to be crossing the Forth Rail bridge on our way into Fife.

I drove my Auntie Agnes to distraction at times. I have always been a curious person and would become fascinated by a particular item in her home which I knew I shouldn't touch. As my hands would reach out almost by themselves to feel the texture, I would be overcome by nerves and knock it over, sometimes with disastrous results. Unfortunately, I broke several prized items in this way!

To be honest, I was a clumsy youngster at the best of times and have not changed much in this regard. Being constantly aware of my aunt's eagle eye and feeling the tension emanating from Mum meant I was an accident waiting to happen.

During our visits, Mum would glare at me if I even thought of running around the house or touching anything which fascinated me. It was inevitable therefore, that I was the cause of a few arguments between Mum and my aunt. Sometimes Mum would storm out of the house after her sister made some remark about my clumsiness; my hand protectively clenched in hers. Although I was grateful to leave the situation, I knew I would be in big trouble when we arrived home.

***

Reading Mum's account of the sexual abuse she and, most likely, her sisters suffered, I wondered how I could write about her agonising experience without becoming so angry that writing would be impossible. In order to hold myself together and work, I often had to lay my emotions aside. Writing is such a solitary pursuit, and it seemed to me at the time that remaining somewhat distant was the only way for me do justice to her pain.

Although my family have been incredibly supportive of this writing journey, I have at times become so immersed in it that I've been unable to recognise, accept and process my own emotions. Indeed, walking away from my computer at the end of a particularly painful writing session, I have often had to take a few deep breaths and unclick my clenched jaw. Sometimes my irritability, especially with men, would cause me to lash out. My long-suffering husband gently talked me through those moments many times.

CHAPTER NINE

1939

Mum turned fourteen years old in May 1939. This was a momentous occasion for her; although of course there were never any birthday celebrations in the family, no... it was thrilling because she was now old enough to leave school! The majority of working-class children left school as soon as they reached the legal leaving age of fourteen in those days to begin their working lives. The only exceptions being especially bright children who would sometimes receive a scholarship to attend grammar school or college.

Mum was bursting with excitement when, on the day after her birthday, Bessie sent her off to the labour exchange instead of school. Eagerly, she waited in the long queue until she finally reached the high counter and saw a stern-looking lady frowning down at her. The lady was obviously waiting impatiently for Mum to speak, and, in a timid voice, she squeaked *"Good morning, I'm here to get a job please."*

The woman thrust her hand across the counter towards Mum saying *"Gie me your birth certificate then lass,"* Mum looked up at her in confusion, *"What is that?"* she said. The woman tutted crossly and told her she would need one if she wanted a job, and she should go back home and ask her mother for it. As Mum turned away, she heard the woman call out irritably, *"And dinnae bother coming back withoot it, wastin' my time!'* Mum didn't even know what a birth certificate was, she had never seen one.

When she trudged home and told Bessie what had happened, she was sent to the shop to tell her father about it. When she arrived there, she waited until he finished with a customer and explained why she had come. She noticed his face become rather pale as she spoke, and he appeared flustered as he hustled her out of the door, telling her he would see her after supper.

That night, Mum received the expected summons to the parlour where her father handed her a sealed brown envelope with orders NOT to open it under any circumstances. She was also ordered to give it directly to the woman at the labour exchange and ask her to reseal it before handing it back. She was to go straight home with the envelope and place it immediately onto his desk.

The following morning, she trotted off with the sealed envelope in her hand; about to do exactly as she had been told. Little did she realise how close she was to the document which could finally reveal the truth of her birth. Arriving at the high counter once again, she stood on tiptoes and handed the envelope up to the grouchy woman.

The woman slit it open and ran her eyes across it before picking up her pen and beginning to write in a big black ledger. As she wrote, she spoke aloud saying … *"Sheila Bell*

Rattray … born 26th May 1925" …etc. Mum looked up at her in confusion and bravely said, *"Excuse me, but you have that the wrong way round, my middle name is Rattray, and my surname is Bell,* The woman looked down her pointy nose at Mum and said, *"Dinnae be so stupid, I can read you know, Rattray is your surname, for heaven's sake!"*

Mum stood looking up at her in bewilderment as the woman wrote the remaining details in the ledger, folded the certificate up and placed it back into the now unsealed envelope. She handed it back down to Mum and dismissed her, saying they would be in touch. Clutching the envelope, Mum left the office in a bewildered state and, looking down at her hand, she noticed the envelope was unsealed. In her confusion she had forgotten to ask the woman to seal the envelope and realised she would be in trouble when her father got home and saw it. Strangely... she didn't even think to peek inside! Why didn't she? To me, that just demonstrates how oppressed she was.

When she arrived home, she placed the unsealed envelope on her father's desk as ordered and quietly left the parlour. She couldn't keep her mind from puzzling over the revelation that her legal surname was actually Rattray, and not Bell. In school she had been known as Bell, and she remembered being called Sheila Bell when she was in hospital. Her father also had often called out 'Miss Bell" when he was issuing orders. She couldn't think why her birth certificate, the one she didn't even know existed until now, was written the wrong way around.

She remembered the startling revelation Don had blurted out a couple of years ago, saying she wasn't his sister. Of course, she also remembered her father telling her she was adopted. Yet again, it made her feel different from her siblings. If the surname of her real parents was Rattray, it was another painful reminder that she didn't belong in the family. Surprisingly, she didn't receive any punishment for the unsealed envelope; in fact, her father never mentioned it at all.

***

Mum was allocated a job in the typing pool of a large business in the centre of Edinburgh. She couldn't touch type for peanuts and hadn't even touched a typewriter before her first day. She thought it would be a glamorous job but was dismayed at the amount of time she had to spend plonking at her battered Remington, trying to produce a letter.

After two weeks of wrestling with the darn machine, she was turning out acceptable work, but realised that office work wasn't for her. However, she loved working as it gave her freedom from the restrictions of school and the darkness of the house. Like most people of her generation, she took her sealed wage packet home and gave it to Bessie for board. She received a portion back to pay for clothes, bus fares, stockings, movies, cigarettes etc. There were many chores in the house she was still expected to complete so she was always busy in the evenings and on weekends.

When she first started work, Mum was very shy and kept her head down, working as hard as she could. Obeying instructions and completing tasks was nothing new to her and she did her job as efficiently as possible. One day, toward the end of her first month at work, she felt important when she was singled out from the other girls in the typing pool by Mr McKenzie, one of the senior staff members.

He asked her to go down to the basement store and get a jar of tartan ink for him. Trotting proudly down to the basement she felt very grown up and, using her most sophisticated voice, spoke clearly to the large, jovial looking man behind the counter, *"May I please have a bottle of tartan ink for Mr McKenzie?"* she said. I can only imagine her dismay to see the man double up, guffawing loudly. When the laughter died down, he looked over the counter at her now scarlet face, wiping tears from his eyes.

"Darlin' lassie, there's no such thing as tartan ink, it's just a wee joke," he said, "they're takin' a lend of ye in the office. Now take your wee self back up the stairs."

Seething with anger, face blazing with embarrassment, she slowly mounted the stairs back up to the office. On arrival, she noticed the room had become silent, everyone appeared to be absorbed in some task or other. Swiftly making up her mind, she strode over to Mr McKenzie's desk and saw his eyes were twinkling with barely contained laughter.

Proudly she stood straighter, raised her chin and, using her most posh voice, looked him directly in the eye saying, *"Sorry, Mr McKenzie, they are out of tartan ink at the present. Apparently, you seem to have forgotten to place the order."* Everyone in the room burst into good-natured laughter at her cheeky comment. After delivering her little speech, she turned gracefully and, as though unfazed by the incident, walked back to her typewriter; head held high, a smile plastered across her face while inside she was shaking like a leaf in a gale. Mum's ability to think quickly and turn the situation around endeared her to everyone there and boosted her emerging confidence.

When reading through this particular story in Mum's memories, it's easy for me to see her quick wit and her talent as an accomplished actress shine through. Later, we three kids often noticed her acting 'hoity toity' at times, the switch from her usual self was instant, and she could reduce a person to insignificance in seconds with her quick wit and withering glance. Her strong will, together with her intelligence, sense of humour and sardonic streak often kept her together during difficult times throughout the rest of her life.

We children were afraid of being on the receiving end of one of Mum's tirades, they were legendary in scale! She was the disciplinarian in our family, although we all knew Dad was behind her, as the head of the house. He was quite happy to let Mum dole out the punishment. We would receive a slap, sometimes across the head, and even the belt on our backsides when we were in deep trouble. Personally, I would rather receive a physical punishment than be on the sharp edge of her tongue as her words always wounded me deeply.

Her moods were mercurial, and often we were unsure just who we were dealing with. I remember one of her often used refrains was, *"You just take me for granted."* It was said with a lift of her chin and through pursed lips. Behind her back, unseen, we would roll our eyes, not really understanding what she meant until we were much older.

***

Shortly after beginning her working life, Mum was forced to pay attention to what was going on in the wider world. The wireless was left to play all day in the staff room and the hourly news reports became ever more disturbing. The Irish Republican Army (IRA) had unleashed a terrifying bombing campaign across England, code named the S-Plan, and many cities, including London, Birmingham and Manchester were bombed.

It was also impossible to miss the constant news reports regarding the tension in Europe as Adolf Hitler flexed his muscles; the threat of war was tangible. The word around the office and in daily newspapers was of the Prime Minister, Mr Chamberlain, and his attempt to pacify Hitler. He made deals and brokered pacts with him to gain assurance the Germans would not invade Poland.

While Mum, along with the other young staff members, didn't really understand the gravity of the unfolding disaster, never having lived through a war, the older ones knew only too well. They generally believed Mr Chamberlain was a weakling who would never be able to prevent Hitler from unleashing the 'dogs of war.' They understood the assurances given were empty, and paper agreements meant absolutely nothing to Hitler.

Poland seemed so far away, and in her naivety, Mum couldn't see why Britain would be affected by an invasion. She was soon to find out exactly what it would mean, as Russia and Germany invaded Poland on Friday, the 1st of September 1939.

Two days later, the music from the kitchen wireless was suddenly interrupted by an urgent bulletin. Bessie and

Mum had been preparing the Sunday roast and they both dropped their peeling knives and crowded around the wireless. The Prime Minister's voice entered the room, declaring the terrible news that Britain was, once again, at war with Germany. Bessie left the kitchen immediately and strode across to the parlour, leaving Mum to wonder what would happen now. The 3rd of September 1939 would forever be remembered as a black day.

The next morning the staff room was abuzz with talk, the fear palpable. As she listened to the conversations around her, she began to understand what the war would mean to them. Once again Britain's sons would be leaving her shores in droves, many never to return. Everyday life was about to change drastically for everyone. Her thoughts went to her brothers: would they have to go and fight? Would they return safely?

Mum's father, David Bell, and wife Agnes Bell with Davey and Agnes 1914

Agnes Bell with Davey, Agnes, Margaret and Jimmy 1918

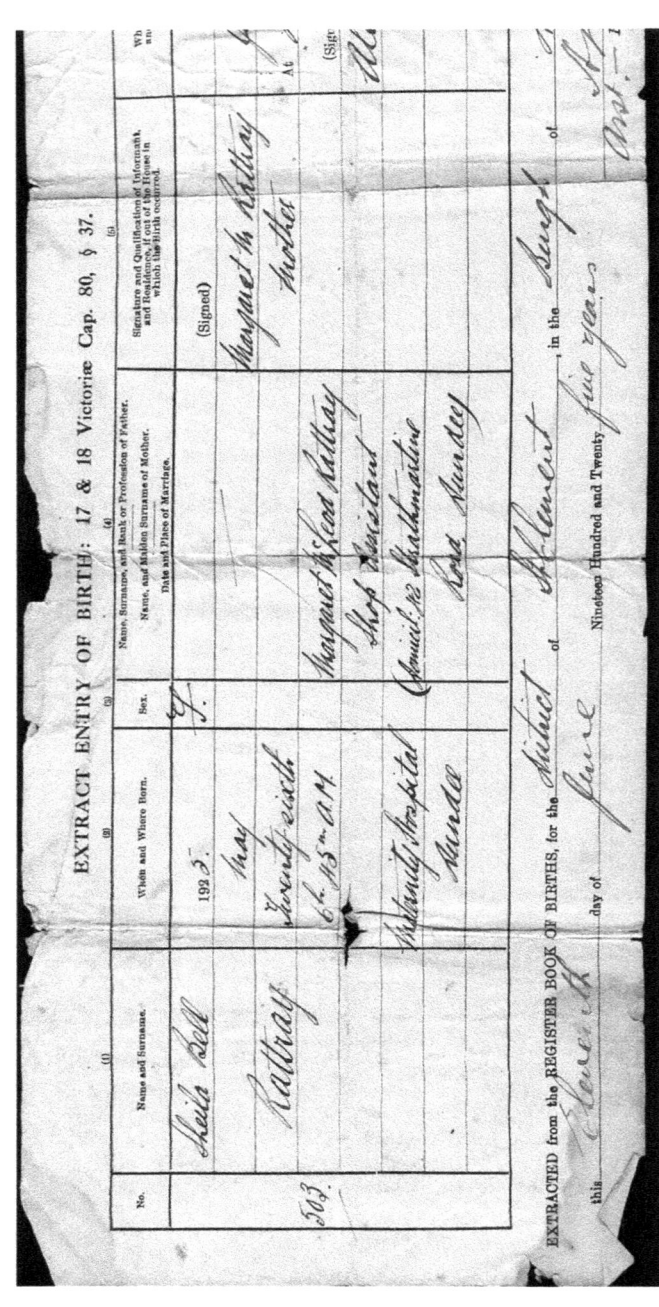

Mum's birth certificate

Mum's father and his new wife Bessie. Wedding photo 1930

Mum's father with Bessie and Mum 1932

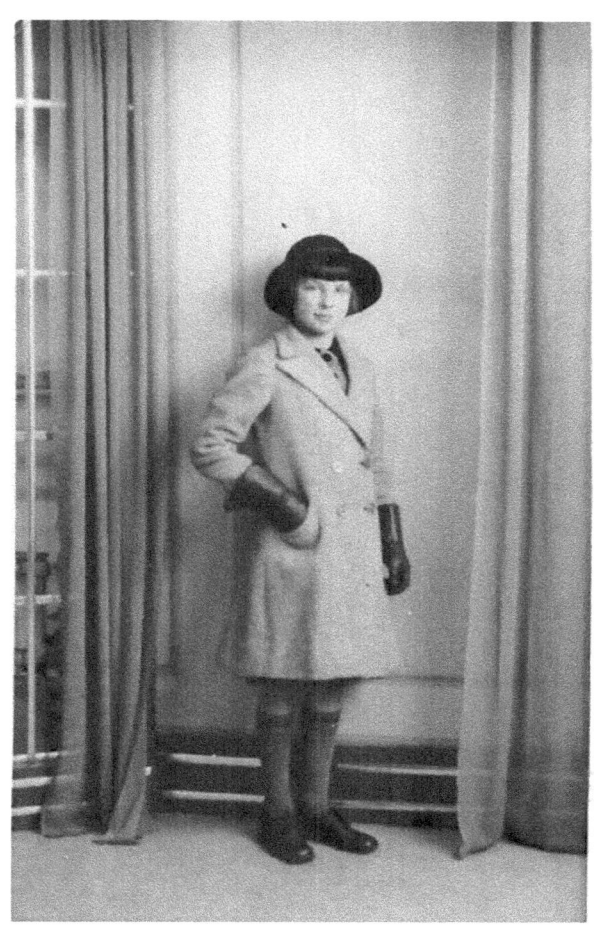

Mum, 1937 aged 12

Mum, 1938 aged 13 before contracting Rheumatic fever

Mum, 1939 after recovering from Rheumatic fever

CHAPTER TEN

1940 - 1943

The war brought death and disaster to so many, however it also brought more freedom and happier times for Mum. In her 'outside of home' life, the self-confidence she had begun to develop continued to flourish and the gangly girl gradually developed into a strikingly beautiful young woman.

She had the grace and carriage of a dancer and was very attractive with her perfect, creamy complexion and dark hair. Her deep blue eyes, shone brightly with life when they weren't flashing with anger and her presence in a room was noticed immediately. In fact, people often remarked on her strong resemblance to Vivien Leigh, a popular British actress of the time.

After more than a year in the office, she knew typing would never be for her. She would never be a good typist and her problems with spelling and grammar didn't help. She decided to make a change and plucked up enough courage to apply for a job in a city shoe store.

The experience she gained from working in her father's store for years paid off, and she started the new job a month later. The store environment was something she really enjoyed; she was so much happier serving customers than she had been tied to a desk all day.

The advent of war swiftly brought about changes at home. She rarely saw her father as he was regularly out of the house in the evenings, doing his bit for the war effort as expected, taking shifts fire watching or as a member of the home guard. On the evenings he was home, she tried to ensure that she was rostered on for fire watch.

Although the nights in the high watchtower were frequently freezing cold, she was happy to be huddled up in her blanket alongside the other volunteer on shift. With a bit of chatter, a flask of tea and sandwiches to pass the night away, she found it quite fun.

***

As a fifteen-year-old working woman, Mum was now given permission to attend the local dance hall with her girlfriends on Wednesday and Saturday nights; with a strict 11pm curfew. She absolutely LOVED to dance! While she was dancing, she felt that she could be who she wanted to be: a carefree young woman, living in the moment. 1940's big band music always sets my imagination afire, and I can't help picturing Mum at one of the dances. Her carefully chosen second-hand frock swirls around her slim legs, browned with fake tan, lines drawn carefully up the back to mimic seams.

Her bright red lipstick frames her wide smile, and her blue eyes sparkle with joy as she circles the dance floor. How she would have dazzled! Waltzing, jiving or jitterbugging along with the music took her to her heavenly place! The girls danced with each other much of the time but also with the boys and young men who attended, often after having a pint or two for courage. Many of the men were on leave from the forces and so glad to be twirling a girl around the dance floor.

Those were heady times for young people as movies and dance halls helped to keep the nation's morale high, it was a way of forgetting reality for a while. Constantly busy beforehand, her life now became a whirlwind of work, chores, dancing, and the occasional movie; she was always on the go.

Very often a young man who had taken a couple of turns around the dance floor with her would offer to see her home, but she generally thanked them and refused. She would rather catch the tram home alone, or at least part of the way with a girlfriend. There had been a few occasions when a fellow would accompany her because he lived close by, and she was careful to say a hasty goodnight at the front door.

She had a couple of experiences saying goodbye to a young man who was not satisfied with the customary handshake or quick kiss on the cheek and expected far more from her. On those occasions, she had sent them on their way quick-smart! As I mentioned earlier, she didn't like to be touched, especially by men.

With the Kirknewton Air Base close by, the American servicemen had begun to appear in Edinburgh early in 1942, almost immediately after the Japanese bombing of Pearl Harbour forced President Roosevelt's hand. The USA had been sending military supplies to Britain since 1940, although there was no appetite in the USA to become any further involved. However, the destruction of nineteen naval ships, the damage or loss of three hundred planes and thousands of men galvanised the US population and the Senate voted unanimously to join the allies.

Although the 'yanks,' as the American boys were dubbed, were brash, confident, and funny, often bringing silk stockings or perfume for the girls, Mum didn't allow any of them to see her home. Of course, many girls were only too happy to go with the cheerful young yanks and countless serious romances were born at the Palais and other dance halls across the country, leading to sixty thousand young women heading to America as GI brides at the close of the war.

Mum became quite good friends with some of the young men she met at the dancing, including a few Americans whom she found to be confident, bright and outgoing. Many of these young men would ask if they could write to her when their leave finished and she was more than happy to agree, giving them the address of the local corner shop.

Mrs McAllister, the storekeeper, held her mail there and many young servicemen wrote to her regularly, telling her about their girlfriends, wives or families or the places they had seen. She loved receiving their letters and wrote back to them faithfully. Whenever she popped into the shop and found a letter there, she would read it out to the kindly shopkeeper, and they would chuckle together at a funny story or feel sad for a boy whose heart had been broken.

The shop cared for Mum's mail because her father routinely searched her room when she wasn't home and would even riffle through her handbag if she left it lying around. One wonders if he was so jealous and controlling, he thought she totally belonged to him? After all, she was the child he tried to throw out of a window as a tiny toddler! He was forever sneaking around as though trying to catch her doing anything of which he disapproved. She didn't understand what he was looking for other than seeking any old excuse to be angry with her - not that he ever needed a reason.

As the years went on, she continued to live a double life, being one person at work, on the dance floor, or out with her friends, and a totally different person at home. Forever guarded and on edge when in the house, even though she was now a young woman, Mum faithfully did her chores and met her curfew. She had to be continuously alert to the mistakes which would give her father an excuse to release his rage on her.

Despite being so careful to be home before curfew, one night she narrowly missed her usual bus and unlocked the door a little past eleven. She had her own key now. When she tip-toed inside, she was shaken to see him standing in the middle of the hall, clearly waiting for her. She felt her stomach turn over and her knees begin to tremble as she was captured by his stare, *"And where have you been,"* he yelled, pushing his watch into her face. Apologising for being late, she stumbled out her explanation of the narrowly missed bus and having to wait for the following one ten minutes later.

It was clear he didn't believe her, as he stepped back to allow his eyes to move up and down her body, contempt and disgust masking his face as he said, *'I suppose you've come home with your belly full."* Her skin crawled with disgust!

She had no intention of letting any man touch her after what HE had done to her.

Thankfully, she didn't react by saying anything to make things worse as she was quite speechless. Afterwards he turned away, dismissing her with a flick of his hand. Only too happy to comply, she headed straight to her room, aware of an unclean, disturbing feeling washing over her because of the way his eyes had taken possession of her body.

***

With so many young men fighting in the war, those left at home did what they could for the war effort while worrying and praying for their sons, fathers and brothers. Mum especially missed her brother Don after he enlisted when he turned eighteen, and they wrote to one another often. She was waiting impatiently for the day when she would turn eighteen and enlist in the Women's Royal Naval Service (WRNS) or the Women's Auxiliary Air Force (WAAF). This would mean she would be doing her bit for the war while being posted far away from home and her father, thereby killing two birds with one stone.

To top it off, the uniforms looked so sophisticated, and she couldn't wait to don her own. On the day she turned eighteen, she applied to the Ministry of Defence and waited impatiently to receive her notice to attend the base hospital for a health check. "*All good*"... she thought as she walked into the clinic.

Unfortunately, she was devastated when the doctor listened to her heart and shook his head, before signing a form to exclude her from service. The rejection meant she had to be content with remaining at home, doing her bit by fire watching and helping with as many fund-raising activities as possible.

Despite this setback, Mum's confidence continued to develop; she was enjoying both work and her busy social life. She loved catching up with the latest movie and was working hard and generally enjoying life as a young woman. She and her best friend Maisie would often spend Saturday afternoons browsing the charity shops; there were so many bargains to be found, often top-quality clothes which they could afford to buy on their small wages.

Many years later Mum would advise us to "Just buy one good quality item, you can dress it up or down or alter it when you want to; it will last you for years," and "Never turn your nose up at decent second-hand clothes." All through her life, she dressed stylishly, even when she was gardening, adding a scarf or pearls to her outfit, but I'm afraid I drove her nuts with my disregard for fashion, preferring jeans and t-shirts to dresses.

CHAPTER ELEVEN

1943 - 1945

Since the outbreak of the war, Bessie had opened the house up to accommodate boarders. Men were sometimes exempt from the services due to being essential workers or because of their ill health or age. They were often required to relocate to the city to take up the jobs left vacant by those in the services. Bessie had been quick to see the opportunity this presented and offered full board to these men, filling the spare bedrooms in the house.

As she provided meals, she held their ration books, and this allowed her to buy extra rationed groceries such as sugar, butter, and eggs. She was also an expert at getting what she wanted on the black market, knowing where to go and who to ask. By hook or by crook, she would manage to get what she wanted.

Generally, the boarders were middle aged and lived in the house only during the working week, heading home on weekends. They were mostly quiet and respectful and did not cause too much disturbance in the running of the house, although their presence did add to Mum's workload.

They chatted pleasantly with her as she served their meals or cleared the table in the evenings, but she usually tried to keep these conversations short. Sometimes they were glad of the chance to share stories of their families at home.

For four nights of the week, she would be in a rush to leave the house to attend to her fire watching duties or meet with her girlfriends to go to a movie or a dance. Some of these friends were working in the munitions factories and a few others were helping on the local farms as everyone pitched in for the war effort. No matter what kind of work they did, they treated each other as equals; all doing their bit.

After an exceptionally cold and dull winter, even by Scottish standards, the first day of spring 1944 brought with it some longed-for sunshine and, more importantly news of some allied victories. Perhaps the fortunes of war were turning around? The morning also brought the arrival of an unexpected new boarder to the house. The first thing Mum noticed about the new man was his age, he appeared to be younger than the others, perhaps in his mid to late twenties. He was friendly and chatted animatedly with everyone at the evening meal. He was enjoying his new carpentry job in Edinburgh and his jovial chatter brought a sunny energy to the table.

With a disarming smile, he introduced himself to Mum, with a light bow in her direction, simply as Tommy. She thought he was rather good looking, with bright blue eyes which sparkled with barely suppressed laughter and thick dark hair. Over the next few days, she began to look forward to a little light-hearted chatter in the evenings as she served or cleared the table; his cheeky banter and infectious laughter brightened the dull dinner conversation.

A few weeks after Tommy's arrival, she carried the dirty dishes into the kitchen to wash and was surprised to hear Bessie speak to her while she worked. Normally the kitchen was a silent place when dinner was over, as Bessie would sit by the kitchen fire to read or settle in the parlour with her father to listen to the wireless. *"Och, that new lad Tommy is really helpful,"* she ventured, *"he's going to make me a new wooden umbrella stand for the front hall."*

During the next month or so, she wouldn't miss an opportunity to tell Mum how nice Tommy was. During the evenings he often popped into the kitchen to chat with Bessie. He seemed lonely and frequently mentioned that he didn't know anyone in the city other than the old fellows at work. Eventually he asked Bessie if she thought Mum would allow him to tag along to the dancing with her so he could meet other people of his own age. When she was asked to invite him, Mum was happy to do so, as she quite enjoyed his lively presence and wondered why she had neglected to ask him herself.

The following Saturday evening they took the tram to the Palais in Fountainbridge. It was Mum's favourite place, most of her friends made their way there at every opportunity as they always featured the best big bands in town. When they arrived, the ballroom was packed as usual with breathless couples waltzing around the dance floor, skirts swirling, and faces flushed. Around the sides of the room there were chairs placed against the walls where girls would sit out a dance or two to catch their breath and giggle, their eyes often on one boy or another.

Tommy was happy to be introduced to her girlfriends and for the next hour or so he had a few girls up on their feet, whirling around the floor in his arms. After a while he asked Mum for a dance, and they stepped onto the floor together for a waltz.

He held her just right in his arms, not too tightly as some of the fellows did, and she relaxed with him as they swept around the room. He turned out to be a lovely dancer and knew all the latest steps which made dancing with him good fun, unlike stumbling through a dance with some of the boys she had danced with who possessed 'two left feet'.

He was a perfect gentleman all evening, making sure he danced with many of the young women there as well as taking a few turns around the floor with Mum again. Some girls cast surreptitious glances her way a few times, envious she was there with such a good-looking chap.

They both thoroughly enjoyed the evening, only leaving reluctantly when she reluctantly explained her curfew to him. Outside in the cooler air, they found themselves chuckling over a joke or two they had heard at the dance and their trip home was filled with chatter. Tommy's impersonations of some of the characters in his small town had her giggling like a schoolgirl as they walked down Easter Road from the bus stop.

On arriving home, Tommy opened the door with his key and ushered her inside, like a gentleman. They stopped in the hallway to say goodnight, and Mum became nervous, she wasn't sure what to do. On the rare occasion she had allowed a chap to walk her home, she would thank them and say goodnight outside, on the doorstep with a quick shake of the hand or a kiss on the cheek and a smile before stepping indoors.

Now, standing in the dim hallway with this young man, she didn't know quite how to end the evening. Tommy looked at her for a second before taking her hand and shaking it, whispering *'Sheila, you're so lovely, I've never danced with anyone as good as you, thanks for a grand night."* Then he turned away and walked off in the direction of his room.

Relieved, she let out the breath she had been holding, and waltzed into her bedroom. While she cleaned her face, she couldn't help smiling at her reflection in the mirror. Sleep evaded her for a while, as she cosied up under the blankets and went over the perfect night in her mind, until eventually falling into a deep sleep with a small, satisfied smile on her face.

The year flew by quickly with hopeful news from the war front trickling in daily from the staffroom wireless. June the 6th, 1944, was D Day, and the huge operation launched a protracted invasion of Normandy, pushing the German troops into retreat. Although this news was encouraging, the human cost was dreadful.

Already, this war had been the deadliest military conflict in history with the death toll among the British troops extremely high. The number of casualties was staggering, and almost everyone knew of a friend, son, husband or father who had been killed or injured by that time. Those with loved ones in the services lived constantly with the dread of receiving a black bordered telegram, notifying them of a death. Apart from her brothers, Mum worried for her pen pals who were still fighting in Europe and Africa; keeping them in her nightly prayers to a God she wasn't sure existed.

The civilian casualties had also reached incredible heights, with over 40,000 being killed in the nine-month bombing blitz of London in May 1941 alone. The Nazi bombing continued unabated, with many other cities also bombarded with death from the skies; and the toll kept rising. People had no choice but to go about their daily lives, supporting the war effort in whatever way they could.

Living without many food items such as onions, sugar, butter, coffee and the like wasn't fun, but it was seen as a small price to pay. Everyone was praying the war would be over soon and they began to imagine their loved ones returning home in one piece.

Tommy and Mum continued to head off to the dance hall together on the occasional Saturday night and would usually take a few turns together on the dance floor before heading home. It was 'the done thing' in those days to dance with many partners during an evening and a girl was thought to be rude if she refused when a fellow asked her to dance with him.

Mum found that she looked forward to the evenings she spent with Tommy, she enjoyed his company, and he was hilariously funny. Laughing came so easily to her on those evenings, his jokes and outlandish stories always left her giggling like a silly girl. Like most young people, she threw herself into enjoying any precious moment which presented itself as it took her mind off the constant worry for her brothers' safety.

There was a new sensation of optimism in the air as hope blossomed along with the progression of summer, leaving the dark days behind. The Normandy landing had swung the tide of war in their favour. With the Russian troops making significant advances through Eastern Europe towards Germany, the allies were pushing their way westerly through France, creating a 'pincer' effect. Talk in corner shops, churches, living rooms and staff rooms, or wherever people gathered, took on an optimistic tone as the summer progressed; after five years of war, loss, and deprivation, they could finally believe it was coming to an end.

As late autumn brought biting north winds and rain, Mum and Tommy returned from dancing one Saturday night and, pushing through the front door, shook the rain from their coats before turning to say goodnight, giggles still rising in their throats. As they stood in the dark hallway, barely repressing their laughter, Tommy whispered, *"May I kiss you."* Surprised, Mum took a breath or two and replied nervously *"Yes, but only a kiss,* softening her words with a smile.

He leaned in, his breath caressing her face, and kissed her softly on the lips; it felt heavenly! He kissed her softly once more, before standing back to gaze into her eyes her hands softly held in his. She was about to say goodnight and turn away towards her room when he suddenly reached out and gripped her tightly around the waist, pulling her roughly against his body, and running his hands down to her bottom, pressing her into his erection. Fear gripped her throat!

***

His kiss, so gentle before, was now bruising her lips against his. Terrified, she pushed him away angrily and whirled away to head towards her room, but he grabbed her arm and spun her back around to face him. Eyes wide, he apologised profusely, trying to grab her hands to hold her there, and begging her forgiveness. "*Your kisses made me lose control of myself,*" he said, and promised her it would never happen again.

"*No, of course it won't*" she said angrily, eyes flashing, "*because I won't be going anywhere with you again.*" With that retort, she turned sharply on her heel and stormed into her room; her face burning with anger and outrage. Once again, she was sleepless, but this time it was her fury keeping her awake; she was so angry he had ruined their friendship.

The following day as she served the Sunday roast, Mum wouldn't look at Tommy, who sat sheepishly at the table while she remained cool and distant towards him. Over the following months, the bitter winter closed over the city and her icy feelings towards Tommy remained. Neither Bessie nor any of the other boarders currently staying in the house commented about this change in her manner towards him, but over the next few months, she became increasingly exasperated at the praises Bessie heaped on her regarding Tommy. "*Such a good laddie*" she would say, or "*See that Tommy, he's a grand one he is.*" He continued to make new things for her.

In the meantime, Mum went dancing with her friends as usual, a little sad in one way he wasn't there to dance with her; they had danced so well together. When her friends asked her where he was, she waved their queries away with vague excuses.

***

New Year's morning 1945 dawned with much optimism across the country, the liberation of Paris the previous August had spurred on the feelings of hope. The newsreels at the cinema and broadcasts on the wireless described battles won and Nazi retreats as the allies' clawed back territory, liberating large swathes of Europe. The bitter winter had decimated the German troops on the Eastern Front, with the Russian troops claiming victory after victory over their former allies.

The war had caused the deaths of so many young servicemen. Even nurses, who were only there to care and heal, had been murdered in cold blood or captured in the Pacific region. Along with the hope it would all end soon, many harrowing stories of atrocities and death came out in the newspapers. This was especially so when the concentration camps were liberated and the full scale of the horrors there became evident.

As spring arrived, optimism rose with the sunshine; the world was weary with mourning.

***

On the afternoon of Tuesday the 8th of May 1945, 'VE' day, Mr Churchill announced across the airwaves that the war in Europe had come to an end. People across the country left their desks, homes or factories and poured out into the streets to dance, drink and celebrate together, a celebration which lasted the whole night for many. While a wave of euphoria washed over the country, it was also a bitter-sweet time for those who had lost loved ones.

At the end of the broadcast, Mum rushed to join the crowds in the street as soon as the shop doors closed. She was caught up in the crazy mood, twirled around and hugged by people whose eyes were filled with tears and laughter. She danced through the streets, never wanting the moment of pure joy to end. Her brothers were safe, and she would see them again soon! Although the war was not over in the far east, it was believed Japan would surrender soon.

The following Sunday, the atmosphere was still infected with euphoria and most people carried on their lives with a new spring in their step. When Mum walked into the kitchen to begin lunch preparations, Bessie told her Tommy had been pleading with her over the last week to ask Mum to go dancing with him again. With the war over, the servicemen would slowly be returning to their jobs and the boarders, including Tommy, would soon be heading back to their own homes.

Keeping Tommy onside was important to Bessie as he was currently working on a bedside cabinet for her, and she wanted to make sure he finished it before leaving. At first Mum was reluctant, she had been keeping her distance from him since he had become too handy with her, but her anger had cooled now. It was impossible not to be softened by the collective confidence sweeping the country, so she agreed.

After all, he was enjoyable company and a lovely dancer, and she was sure he must have learned from his earlier mistake. Over the next few days, she secretly felt pleased he had asked again; he would certainly be off home to his wee village soon and was surely looking to enjoy his last few months in the big city.

Saturday night arrived. Mum was waiting nervously in the hall and when Tommy came from his room, she glanced at him with a slight smile before leading the way out the door. On their trip to the Palais, Tommy was an absolute gentleman, and she was able to relax in his company once again. They were soon chatting non-stop, and she found herself laughing, once again, at his outlandish jokes.

They spoke of the friends and loved ones who would shortly be making their way home from the war and how much they looked forward to life going back to normal again. Of all her brothers, Mum had especially missed Don, and she was looking forward to having him settled back into the house, so she told Tommy a few funny tales about her big brother.

During the evening Tommy asked her to dance with him several times and it was obvious they still danced well together; Mum was over the moon with happiness. He paid particular attention to her all evening and whispered of her beauty as they swept around the room; she lapped it all up. They left the dance hall arm in arm, eyes sparkling, still dizzy from their last waltz and hurried to catch the bus.

Arriving home, they stepped into the hallway and Tommy asked Mum if he could kiss her. With a little smile, she whispered a yes; but … *"No hanky-panky, OK?"* she said. He laughingly agreed and leaned towards her brushing his lips over hers softly and lightly and she felt herself melt with the gentleness and warmth of his embrace.

After this most gentle and chaste of kisses, he turned away saying, *"Goodnight beautiful"* and disappeared into his room. She was over the moon and felt like a princess while preparing for bed, humming the latest tunes to herself and smiling into the mirror. She felt she was as beautiful as he said she was, the sparkle in her eyes turning them sapphire blue. She twirled a few times around her room, her nightgown billowing around her legs and collapsed into bed where she fell into a dreamy, sound sleep.

***

Sometime during the night, she was abruptly snatched out of her sweet dreams by the sensation of someone climbing into her bed. Panicking, she tried to sit up, but the dark shape held her down and her whole body froze, the scream in her mind unable to escape from her throat. In her childhood, she had frozen when her father molested her and her body and soul froze, as they had learned to do before.

It took only a split second to fall into the same protective state she had unconsciously used as a child, and she felt herself floating outside her frozen body. It was only when she could numbly observe the scene unfolding below her that she realised what was happening, too late.

Despite the dark, she realised, it was Tommy and not her father who was crushing her vacant body beneath him, cruelly raping her! With her body still frozen in fear, she lay as motionless as a statue, unable to scream or move while he took what he wanted from her.

It was all over quickly, and Tommy rolled off her stumbling to his feet, pyjama pants clutched in one hand, mumbling *"I'm so sorry, I couldn't help myself; I love you so much and I want to marry you."* Coming back into herself now his weight was lifted from her, she grabbed the blankets and clutched them up to her chin before quietly and coldly, through her chattering teeth, ordering him to "Get out!"

When she was sure he had gone from the hallway, she rose and edged quietly, painfully, to the bathroom where she drew a scalding hot bath and scrubbed her damaged body, trying to remove all trace of him. When her body was red raw, she lay in the rapidly cooling bath. She shed no tears and felt no anger, only repulsion, her body and soul were hollowed out as though she was an empty shell.

In the morning she rose and spent the day carrying out her normal Sunday chores, before sitting by the kitchen fire catching up on her embroidery as though nothing had happened. She was blank. When suppertime came, she served the boarders without acknowledging her rapist in any way, the protective barrier with which she had surrounded herself locked resolutely in place.

The following day, she continued to act as though nothing had happened and left the house to go to work; after all, she was used to keeping secrets locked inside her wounded soul. As she worked through the day, she made up her mind to put the horror to the back of her mind and get on with her life and, over the next few days, managed to tuck her emotions into the brimming vault of pain within. As the year crept on, she still served meals as she had before the rape but continued to blank him as though he did not exist.

She continued with her double life, a façade of confidence carrying her through her outside life and remaining her usual silent and subservient self at home. Late at night, as she tried to sleep, she struggled with the feelings of shame, disgust and guilt which plagued her; she was so angry with herself for not screaming or fighting when she awoke with Tommy holding her down. It was a huge struggle to pull her shoulders back and smile bravely each morning as she closed the door behind her, tilted her chin up, and stepped into the city streets to face the day. Mask firmly in place!

***

As a child, I think I intuitively recognised that Mum had at least two distinct sides to her. Her ability to face the world, to survive, following everything that had happened to her in her short twenty years of life is incredible. The ability to act as different people: a silent, obedient, and robotic presence at home and a bright, confident young woman who could laugh and dance with her friends when outside, astounds me. I became acutely aware as I grew older that she was a better actress than Grace Kelly, whom she resembled with her beauty and grace.

***

When I was growing up, I never knew which person would be greeting me when I came into the house and was always a little on edge travelling home, somehow expecting trouble.

I viewed her as the most powerful person in our family, a real force to be reckoned with, but I also sensed a vulnerability tucked inside.

As her story of rape leaps off the page through her handwriting, my understanding of the complex, damaged woman who bravely chose to tell her story produces in me such awe. As I write of this horrifying time, I see her in my mind's eye, lifting her chin up again and again as she steps out of the house. I am left filled with tears too deep to release, my heart breaking.

CHAPTER TWELVE

1945

Although the country was still jubilant over the end of such a long war and looking forward to happier times, an early autumn came bowling in with a vengeance. Everyone hurriedly aired out their winter woollies or used up their precious clothing rations to buy a warm coat. One evening, as Mum carefully pressed her three heavy woollen skirts and her winter blouses, she decided that she would visit her favourite charity shop to look for a new coat. In her mind, she counted her pennies.

The following morning, she climbed into one of her newly pressed skirts, only to discover it was noticeably tighter than when she had last worn it, so she tried on the remaining skirts, only to find them both the same. It was obvious she had put on a fair bit of weight over the last few months, and she realised that something wasn't right with her. Never having been one to time her periods, she let her thoughts drift back over the past months and realised how much time had flown by since her last one, so much had happened lately.

Tommy's attack on her had followed closely on the elation of the war's end, and she simply hadn't noticed the absence of her 'monthlies.' Nevertheless, she put her missing periods down to these dramatic events and packed any other thoughts away to the back of her mind.

Don arrived home on shore leave from the navy a few days later and, overjoyed to see him safe and sound, she wrapped her arms around him tightly in an unusual show of affection and relief. He laughed loudly and twirled her around, holding her at arm's length to see her better. As she stood before him, he flippantly mentioned *"Oh, it was alright for you at home, eating up and getting chubby."* Mum chuckled along with him as she turned to put the kettle on for a cuppa, but the chuckle died on her lips when it dawned on her that the snugness of her skirts could mean something too appalling to contemplate.

The next afternoon, as they were in the kitchen and the house was quiet, Bessie stopped her on her way out the door and asked, *"You're no expectin,' are you?"* Mum knew what the word *expecting* meant, it was usually whispered between women as they gossiped together; it meant the person being murmured about was going to have a baby. Her sister Agnes already had a lovely little boy, and Margaret was 'expecting' another wee one too.

Ducking her head in shame and fear, her carefully constructed barrier to the truth collapsed and she crumpled into the fireside chair, sobbing uncontrollably. Bessie crossed her arms over her ample bosom and stood before the fire, tapping her foot, waiting for an explanation. When her voice was steady enough, Mum blurted out the appalling truth she had been raped by Tommy, Bessie's precious boarder.

Tight lipped, Bessie stared at her for a while and began to pace around the kitchen; she was obviously in a flat spin, twisting her hands together and sighing. Slumped in the chair, not knowing what to do or say, Mum just felt disbelief at what was happening to her! What was to become of her now? She was terrified her father would beat her and send her to a Mother and Baby home when he found out. It was as though her brain wouldn't work; she didn't know what to do.

Later that evening, she discovered that Tommy had come home from work and Bessie had spoken to him about Mum's condition, giving her version of events. Coward that he was, Tommy wasted no time; he escaped by climbing through his bedroom window, suitcase in hand.

The following morning, following a sleepless night tossing and turning with her mind in a turmoil, Mum walked to a telephone box to inform the shop manager that she was ill. After stepping back through the front door, she headed straight to her room and curled around herself on the bed, wondering what would become of her. As she lay there, tears raining ceaselessly from her eyes, Bessie opened her door to say she was going into the city to see someone and pick up a few groceries. Alone now, trapped in a jumble of thoughts, she felt there was no answer to her situation, and came to a swift decision.

Rising from the bed, she marched into the parlour, collected all the newspapers in there and closed both the kitchen door and window. In a sudden flurry of activity, she rolled the newspapers up and stuffed them under the door and into the gaps around the wooden window. She crossed to the cooker and turned all the gas knobs to their highest setting.

With her heart racing, she knelt before the oven and turned its dial right around to its highest setting. She didn't light anything. She leaned forward and put her head right inside the deep oven, sucking deep breaths of the poisonous gas into her throat, already raw from crying. Trying not to cough, she waited and prayed to die; she was too ashamed to live! It didn't take long for her body to slither silently down, and she lay motionless on the kitchen floor.

At some stage, she became aware that she could hear someone coughing and gagging and felt herself being dragged across the floor. She opened her eyes and realised Bessie was pulling her through the open kitchen door and into the hallway. She dropped her there, face up and plonked down onto the floor next to her, wheezing loudly. Mum was retching dreadfully and felt tears streaming down her face, wetting her hair. She turned over as the retching became worse and she vomited all over the floor.

She lay in her own mess, sobbing, she was terribly ill. When Bessie had recovered sufficiently, she helped her into the bathroom and Mum cleaned herself up a bit before collapsing into bed with a bucket next to her head. As she lay on the bed, overwhelmed with dread and misery, she puzzled over why she was alive; there was nothing to live for after all.

The following day Mum found out how she had been saved from certain death. Bessie had walked up the street to catch the bus to the city, but the clear morning had suddenly turned grey, and a heavy shower caused her to duck into the corner shop at the top of the road to wait for the rain to pass. While there, she spent some time gossiping with the shop-keeper and a few neighbours who were also sheltering there, before peeking out the door and realising the bad weather had set in for the day.

She made up her mind to buy a few essentials for the evening meal in the corner store and travel into the city the following day. Decision made; she scuttled home in the downpour and found Mum close to death. Afterwards, Mum wondered whether it had been Edinburgh's famously change-able weather which saved her life or whether her saviour had been the God she struggled to believe in?

***

A few days after her failed suicide attempt, Mum was still in bed and slowly recovering, when Bessie handed her a thick, sealed envelope. There was an address on the front written in unfamiliar handwriting and Mum looked at her, confused. Bessie told her to get her coat on and *"Take yersel away doon to this place and they will help ye oot."* Intrigued and yet puzzled, Mum hoped her stepmother's words meant something could be done to help her.

She struggled aboard a bus and then took a tram, getting off at a street close to the place she was supposed to go. Bent over against the freezing November wind, she found the right street and slogged all the way down to the end. It was dark and dank. She stood before a grey tenement building, staring at it in confusion; this place didn't look anything like the office she had been expecting to arrive at. The door to the stairwell was closed, its black peeling paint revealing the rotting wood underneath.

Pushing hard on the heavy door and entering the lobby, she was instantly assailed by the sickening smell of old cooking fat, mixed with who knows how many years' worth of dried piss. She squinted down at the envelope in the dim light to see the flat number and clambered up the cold concrete stairs to the second floor. Standing on the landing, she stared around her in dismay at the floor littered with rubbish.

With a trembling hand, she knocked on the appointed door. A tall, stout, middle-aged woman answered and hastily bustled her into a dark hallway. Taking the envelope out of Mum's shaking hand, she closed the door firmly behind her and ushered her into a room which was furnished like a doctor's examination room. Mum sat tensely in the patient's chair as instructed by the woman, and looked around her, thinking that the room didn't fit her idea of a surgery, she had never seen one so disorderly and threadbare.

After an anxious wait, a tall, silver haired man came bustling through the door wearing a harassed expression. It was obvious he was a doctor, as he was wearing a white coat and had a stethoscope slung carelessly around his neck. Without offering his name, he gruffly told Mum to take her coat off and proceeded to listen to her chest through the stethoscope, murmuring "*cough ... big breath*" etc.

When he finished his brief examination, he shook his head and straightened up to his full height, brusquely telling her there was nothing he could do for her, *"No wi a heart like that, lass!"* After this announcement, he turned from her dismissively and stomped out of the room.

A minute later, the stout woman swished through the door and shoved the envelope back into Mum's hands, then pushed her out the door and back onto the filthy landing. Much later in her life, she was horrified to realise she had almost had an abortion and was glad, for once, for the heart condition that prevented it.

The next day she rose from a nap in her room and headed through the hallway intending to help with the lunch preparations when she heard voices in the kitchen. Standing outside the kitchen door to listen, she heard Bessie, Agnes and Margaret's voices discussing something in fervent, yet subdued tones. She realised they were discussing her pregnancy, and it was clear from their words that their most immediate concern was for her safety.

They were fretting about what may happen to her when their father found out about it. She opened the door and walked into the kitchen and all three turned toward her in surprise. Her sisters stepped closer to hug her, and Bessie left them together to talk. She broke down, enveloped in their rare embrace, and sobbing, told them how the pregnancy had happened. The reality of the way Tommy had come into the bedroom in the dead of night to rape her came spilling out. They were shocked by her revelation.

An angry look passed between her sisters as she spoke, they pursed their lips, disgust on their faces. They told Mum Bessie had given them a totally different explanation of how she became pregnant. Saying she didn't know who the baby's father was and insinuating he could have been any number of men.

Mum was relieved that her sisters believed her; they knew Bessie often twisted the facts for her own benefit. They were furious, not only with Tommy, but also with their stepmother for her nasty lie. No one thought to report the rape to the police. After all, who would believe her, even if she could put her shame and guilt aside long enough to speak of it?

Agnes sat Mum down with a cup of tea and took charge as she usually did. She told her to collect herself together, finish her tea and then go and pack a suitcase. She was coming to live with Agnes and her son Billy for now, as there was a spare room in her flat. While Mum was frantically packing, Margaret headed home, and Agnes strode briskly to her father's store to tackle the task of telling him the truth about her little sister's pregnancy. She knew he would not hear the truth from Bessie, who wouldn't want him to know one of her boarders was a rapist.

When Mum walked out of the house, she felt a mixture of hope and relief to be leaving; she didn't look back as she walked up the road, arm in arm with Agnes, suitcase in hand.

***

After telephoning work to say she was ill and unlikely to recover anytime soon, Mum told them to fill her position. She couldn't face going to work and fronting the other girls who would eventually guess her condition, after all it wasn't something that could be hidden much longer. She feared they would judge her harshly. Plucking up all her courage, she wrote a letter to her dear friend Maisie, who still worked there, explaining what had happened to her.

She was relieved to receive a reply by return mail, and in her letter, Maisie wrote of her sorrow and anger at what had been done to her dear friend. Her promise to do anything she could to help Mum was balm to her shattered heart, and she was deeply grateful for her wonderful best friend.

Agnes, being the practical person she was, immediately set about trying to arrange everything for her sister's future. Within a few days of moving Mum in, she went back to Easter Road to ask Bessie for Mum's ration book and, while she was there, she asked for her birth certificate too, realising it may be needed in the coming months.

Bessie sighed and rummaged through her handbag to retrieve Tommy's tattered, light brown ration book, which she handed over grudgingly. The man had obviously been too concerned with escaping to bother about the valuable book. She went into the hallowed parlour and took the certificate from the desk drawer. Back in the kitchen, she handed it to Agnes saying, *"If your faither notices it's gone, I'll tell him it was you who took it."* "Fair enough", Agnes thought, and headed home.

When she settled into her seat on the bus, Agnes retrieved the book from her handbag and quickly spotted that the name scrawled on the front was not Tommy; it appeared his real name was William, and his untidy writing indicated his home address was in a small village to the north of Edinburgh.

When her sister handed Mum her birth certificate, she sat down to finally discover the truth of her birth. As she read through it, she understood the confusion at the labour exchange, as the full name given on the certificate was indeed Sheila Bell Rattray.

Her own mother's name jumped out at her: Margaret McLeod Rattray, she had a mother somewhere. It was with relief she now understood that, although she was illegitimate, she did in fact share the Bell blood with her half siblings and wasn't an orphan, after all. This was rather a defining moment for her; it seemed that she did belong, at least a little.

Agnes's next plan of action was to ensure Tommy was made to take responsibility for his callous, painful, assault on her sister. She planned to make him marry her, or at the very least, financially support this baby of his.

When Agnes spoke to Mum that evening, telling her she must go and see Tommy, as he had to do the right thing and marry her, she adamantly refused. She shouted angrily, *"No, I never want to see that pathetic excuse for a man again and will never marry him!"* However, Agnes continued to insist over the following days, chipping away at her, until her arguments began to make sense. Although there was no way she would ever marry that cruel beast, he should be made to support her baby.

Even thinking about seeing his face again made her want to be sick, nevertheless, she knew she would have to pluck up the courage to go and face him. It was with a heavy heart that she sighed deeply and sat down to write a letter to Maisie, asking if she would go with her for support. Maisie's reply was swift, saying of course she would help her best friend, and they set about making plans for the upcoming weekend.

On Saturday morning, they met at the bus stop to catch the bus north, grasping their thick coats around them for protection from the freezing wind. They were chilled to the core by the time the bus arrived with a squeal of brakes, and they clambered into the relative warmth gratefully.

They sat nervously together, legs stiff and handbags clutched in their white fists, hardly speaking. After an hour lumbering through the countryside, they arrived at the village and stepped down onto the cobbled high street, wondering how they would find the right house. The wind whipped their coats around them as they headed towards a group of shops, hoping to find someone to give them directions.

Peering into the window of a wee shop hoping to see a helpful face, they noticed a woman bending to place something into one of the glass cabinets and decided to step inside. The warmth instantly embraced them, and the woman stood up to beam a warm smile their way.

She was rather elderly and slightly built but was ready for a chat, so they put their ration coupons together and bought a little bag of sweeties from her, a rare treat. Mum asked a few questions about the quaint village and the woman grumbled for a few minutes about the dreadful weather, a favourite pastime of the Scots.

Taking a deep breath, Mum showed her the address she had copied from Tommy's ration book, and the kindly woman said *"Och aye, that'll be Willy's' mother's hoose, it's up the road a wee bit."* Kindly, she stepped out of the warm shop with them, crossing her shawl against the wind, and directed them along the high street towards the end of the village. *"If you walk up the road a way, it's the last hoose on the left, the wee white one."* With nerves aquiver, they set off.

After slogging along for what felt like hours, but was probably only fifteen minutes, they approached the cottage. Mum clenched her hands as she stopped across the road to take in the squat, slate-roofed cottage with a black door and two small windows with clean lace curtains.

They crossed and stood anxiously for a moment before the small gate, Mum's heart hammering in her chest as she stared, sweat breaking out on her brow. She pushed the gate open and stood before the heavy wooden door attempting to catch her breath before knocking. She knocked, hand trembling and her heart in her mouth.

A middle-aged woman opened the door and stood in the tiny hallway, wiping her hands on her apron. Mum noticed immediately she had the same bright blue eyes as Tommy, making her gasp. She realised this woman was Tommy's mother but found herself speechless after her shock. Maisie rescued her by asking to speak to 'William' and the woman peered at them intently for a second or two before she sighed and bowed her head as though in defeat.

Standing back, she ushered them into the sitting room. As she entered the cosy room, Mum's voice returned along with her courage, and she spoke openly of her reason for the disturbance. She was astonished to see that Tommy's mother showed no surprise at her harrowing story.

The woman told her Agnes had written to her son demanding he take responsibility for the rape and the resulting pregnancy. Not knowing what else to say, Mum quietly asked her when 'William' would be home, and his mother began wringing her hands. Obviously upset, she said that he was rarely home these days. Ever since the letter arrived, he had taken to spending every day in the pub, only coming home late at night to stagger into bed.

After blurting this out, her eyes welled up with tears and she became flustered, flapping her apron up and down to cool her face before using it to wipe her eyes. To Mum's shock, she said her son had a wife and a wee three-year-old girl to support and that his wife had become hysterical when she found the crumpled letter from Agnes on the floor and threatened to kill herself.

She had taken her daughter to her mother's place in a nearby town, giving no indication as to if or when they would be back. Horrified at these revelations, Mum turned on her heel to leave, but stopped at the living room door to spin back towards the unfortunate woman, saying angrily, "*Tell his poor wife not to bother killing herself... he's not worth it!*"

After this dreadful visit, Maisie kindly linked arms with Mum as they walked slowly back to the bus stop because she was struggling to see through her tears, unable to hold them back any longer. Glad to leave the village behind them, they rode home silently, too shaken and emotionally exhausted to speak.

When they parted to board their own trams, Mum's tears fell again as she thanked her dear friend for her support.

Maisie would remain Mum's staunch friend for many years and would one day be instrumental in bringing about a major change in her life.

Strangely, there is no mention of Tommy's last name in Mum's writing. It must surely have been written on his ration book, and I find the omission curious. Perhaps she had forgotten it forty years on from that painful time, or perhaps she omitted it for reasons known only to herself? We will never know.

CHAPTER THIRTEEN

1946

The months passed slowly by as Mum awaited the birth of her child. She settled into a calm, peaceful life in her sister's cosy home and helped with the housework and cooking. Walking Billy to and from school was a time she especially enjoyed; his animated chatter kept her from over-thinking. In the evenings, she sat contentedly sewing and embroidering tiny nighties and matinee jackets for her baby.

Margaret knitted the most beautiful, gossamer thin, shawl for her; she was so grateful for her sisters and their support. Over the dark winter months, whenever Agnes had visitors in the flat, she would hide herself away in her bedroom to sew or rest because she was too ashamed of her condition to face people. As the months passed, there was no discussion about what would happen when the baby arrived, and she remained cocooned in a bubble of safety, warmth, and peace.

During this period Agnes was seeing a lovely man, George, who seemed to make her very happy. It was clear from the beginning that he adored her. When he visited the flat for the first time, Agnes coaxed Mum out of her room to meet him.

Mum was delighted to see how loving and respectful he was towards her big sister; she deserved to be happy. He extended the same respect to Mum, even in her current unmarried, pregnant state and didn't appear to pass judgement on her.

During their courtship, he proved himself to be kind and extremely generous. He was a top solicitor who, in addition to his sterling legal career, held the honourable position of High Constable of Holyrood House, which is the Royal Palace in Edinburgh. This prestigious position dates back to the sixteenth century and involves the many ceremonial duties required when the royal family, or someone else of great importance, are in residence at Holyrood. He introduced Agnes into the city's high society, and she blossomed in his adoration.

In early December, George took them all on holiday to the Lake District in England, and they spent a wonderful week together in that magical place. It was the first holiday Mum had ever experienced, and she was captivated by the scenery. The first-class train ride, the posh hotel and the wonderful meals they savoured were heavenly.

She and Billy spent the evenings playing games together to allow the couple time alone, and the days brought lovely walks across the hills in the brisk, late winter air. Mum felt peaceful and secure, and her cheeks glowed with health when they returned home.

With her belly growing bigger every day, it was soon time to head to Simpson's maternity hospital for her pre-natal medical examination. There, after the nurse had fired endless questions her way, she waited to be called for an examination by the doctor. Sitting in the waiting room, she felt extremely uncomfortable as she felt the other women peering furtively at her left hand seeking a wedding ring and she felt terribly embarrassed and ashamed under their disapproving glances.

During the medical examination, the doctor explained that a home birth would be impossible for her, and she was devastated. Most women gave birth at home in those days and here she was, different yet again. He went into detail about the problem with her heart, explaining her mitral valve was leaking because of the damage inflicted by rheumatic fever. She was grateful to him as she finally understood the problem with her heart. There was a high risk to her life during childbirth and more importantly to her, the life of her child. Despite her disappointment she understood and accepted his decision, more than anything, she wanted her baby to be safe.

***

In the early hours of the 3rd of March 1946, Mum was torn from a deep sleep by severe pains in her stomach. She rose and paced around the flat for a couple of hours, leaning over the table when the pains took hold of her. Eventually the pain overcame her fear of going to hospital and she crept into her sister's bedroom to wake her. By this point, she was pale, and sweating profusely so Agnes took control and ran to the telephone box to call for an ambulance.

Mum remembers being whisked straight to the delivery room and strapped into stirrups. After another excruciating pain shredded her to fragments of herself, she noticed a gas tank next to her and remembered her sisters saying that gas helps with the pain. No matter how hard she begged for the mask, they would not give it to her as it was too dangerous with her damaged heart.

She didn't remember much more except grabbing the lapels of a man's dark woollen dressing gown and hearing him shouting at her to push hard. When the unbelievable pains gripped her, she felt as though she was being split in two. Thankfully it was soon all over, and she was told she had a fine baby boy.

With a mixture of joy and relief, her avid eyes followed her baby as he was swaddled and taken from the room. A nurse explained she would see him when the doctor had finished examining him in the nursery, and after a gentle wash, she fell into a deep sleep.

When she awoke, she realised it was early morning and peered out from her bed, wondering what had woken her. There was a faint wailing coming from the corridor. The sound grew stronger, strong enough to discern the cacophony of many babies crying at once. Suddenly, the double swinging doors at the end of the ward crashed open and the sound became deafening.

She struggled upright and watched on in awe, as two nurses pushed a huge trolley, filled on either side with small wire cots, each cot holding a squalling, hungry baby. The nurses lifted each baby in turn and carried it across to the appropriate mother for a feed. The babies looked like little Egyptian mummies, all wrapped up tightly in their white muslin wraps with only their little faces showing.

Mum waited, eagerly watching every baby as it was ferried to its mother, wondering when her empty arms would be filled. Her eyes were sparkling with barely contained excitement, despite her exhaustion, she was finally going to meet her little boy! When the nurse placed the tiny, snugly-wrapped bundle into her arms, she gazed down in awe at his tiny face; amazed that he looked a little like Tommy, with the same chin and dark hair.

Putting all thoughts of Tommy steadfastly out of her mind, she decided never to think of him again. When she put her son instinctively to her breast, as she had seen her sisters do, she felt the deepest love bubbling and sizzling inside her soul and was so proud when he latched on immediately and suckled like a pro. *"Sunday's child is full of grace,"* she thought to herself as she held him close.

She decided to name him Bryan and added the middle name George, in honour of her sister's boyfriend who had been so kind to her over the past months. A feeling of completeness engulfed her, and she felt whole for the first time in her life. Over the rest of the day and the next, she secretly examined every inch of his tiny body with wonderment when he arrived for feeds, even though the mothers were not supposed to unwrap their babies. She marvelled at his long fingers and toes, such a Bell feature, she thought.

Every night, fathers were allowed to visit the ward between seven and eight and when they arrived, Mum hid herself under the blankets; ashamed to have no husband of her own to sit by her bed.

On the third morning after Bryan's birth, she received a visit from a harassed woman who said she was the hospital's Lady Almoner. An almoner was like a social worker in those days, and every hospital in Britain had one. It was immediately obvious to Mum that the woman was angry. Huffing and puffing, she said she had discovered Mum was breastfeeding her baby, and that this unacceptable situation would stop immediately! Once she had dropped this bombshell, she turned away and blustered back out through the swinging doors, leaving Mum in tears of confusion. An hour later, when the 10am feeding parade arrived, nurses with babies in their arms bypassed her bed one by one, leaving her with empty arms and painful breasts.

When all the babies had been distributed and silence had descended on the ward, Mum's favourite nurse came to talk to her. The nurses had been ordered not to allow her to feed her baby, but they hadn't been told why. She was very reassuring, saying that Bryan was being well looked after in the nursery for the time being.

Devastated, Mum buried herself under the blankets and cried herself to sleep. Generally, people did not question those in authority in those days, but perhaps more significantly, she had been conditioned to obey others who had power over her and didn't question the decision further. She spent the next few hours crying and brooding, before determining that the decision must have been made because of her ill health and she just had to accept it.

As she drowsed during that day, she dreamt she could hear Bryan crying for her and felt her painful breasts respond, filling even further with useless milk. Later in the afternoon, a couple of nurses bound her breasts with bandages to stop her milk production. She felt powerless.

In the wee hours of the next morning, Mum was suddenly woken by gripping pains in her stomach and reached for the bell to summon a nurse but began vomiting all over the bed and onto the floor. She was shivering so much it was hard to get a grip on the bell and sweat was trickling down her face. When the night nurse came and saw her state, she quickly swished the bed away to a private room.

There, Mum faded in and out of consciousness, tormented by nightmares. As she awoke, she heard someone frantically calling out Bryan's name and realised it was her. She was calmed by a nurse who was sitting by the bed, preparing to bathe her. As she gently washed Mum, the sympathetic nurse explained that she had been critically ill with childbed fever and had been close to death for days. Hurriedly, she reassured her that baby Bryan was in the nursery and doing very well.

The following two weeks dragged along, with Mum mostly confined to bed in a small ward she shared with an elderly lady. She managed to beg a nurse now and again to wheel her to the nursery window and her heart leapt to see Bryan, sleeping contentedly in his little wire crib. She spent her days sleeping and trying to eat everything that was brought to her to build her strength up. Her heart and her arms ached with emptiness, but she knew she had to get well quickly so that she could be reunited with her baby.

***

Finally, after almost a month in hospital, she was deemed well enough to go home and the big 'leaving' day dawned. She could hardly contain her happiness and dressed clumsily with trembling fingers, she wanted to be ready to leave when breakfast was over. Agnes arrived, carrying a small bag filled with a few fluffy white nappies and some items from the layette for her little son to wear for the trip home.

She placed all the tiny items out on the bed, laying the gossamer shawl which Margaret had knitted over the top, and Mum was ecstatic to imagine her baby boy wrapped up so warmly in the clothes she had sewn. The nurses collected the clothes and dressed Bryan in the nursery and when they returned, they handed him to his mother.

She held him to her heart for the first time in weeks, marvelling, proudly, at how much he had grown already. She held him so close she was afraid she might squeeze him forever, her tears dripping down onto the lovely shawl.

When the nurse wheeled her through the drab hospital corridors and out into the fresh air, her heart rose with joy, which was at odds with the tears coursing down her cheeks. She gazed down into her little boy's eyes and he stared right back, with an inquisitive, searching stare. Although she had been discharged, she was still very weak, and wobbled a little trying to get out of the wheelchair, so Agnes took Bryan from her arms. When she had steadied herself and was safely standing, she clutched him back into her arms quickly.

Nevertheless, as they walked slowly down the path from the hospital, it soon became obvious she wasn't strong enough to hold him safely, and Agnes took him from her shaking arms again. They began the long walk across the paths leading them through the meadows to the tram stop.

After carefully climbing aboard the tram, Mum slumped down, shaking with exhaustion and Agnes sat next to her with Bryan snuggled in her arms. Within minutes, Mum's eyes began to close with fatigue, and when she opened them to peer through the opposite window, she vaguely realised the tram was heading in the wrong direction for home.

She sat up straighter, blinking sleep away, and looked at Agnes quizzically. Seeing her sister was looking calmly ahead, Bryan contentedly asleep in her arms, she dreamily assumed they must be on their way to Margaret's house. She was eager to show her beloved sister the new addition to the family, and with a sigh of relief, settled back to float off into a daze again.

After what felt like only a few seconds, the tram stopped with a squeal of brakes, waking her. Mum didn't recognise the street they stepped down to and asked where they were going. Agnes said they just had to go a little further and they walked slowly along to a gate, which she swung open. Once through the gate, Mum was ushered across a large garden to the door of a grand stone house with bay windows.

Opening the door, they stepped into a bright hallway with a round table in the centre adorned with a large vase full of colourful flowers. There were many doors set around the hallway and Agnes knew exactly which one to knock upon and open. She led Mum into a room where a matronly looking woman stood to greet them warmly, inviting them to take a seat. Mum almost collapsed into a soft leather chair, feeling faint and rather nauseous by this stage. The woman settled herself behind a large oak desk before introducing herself to Mum as Mrs Jenner.

It appeared Agnes already knew her, and Mrs Jenner swiftly proceeded to throw jumbled streams of words into the air, expecting them to be understood. Although her sister kept nodding in agreement with Mrs Jenner, something stopped Mum from understanding their meaning. She felt exhausted, somehow missing the significance of the words as she couldn't seem to make them string together in any coherent sense. It was as though the woman was speaking in a foreign language which Mum was unable to translate and the weight of knowledge floated past her as if it belonged to someone else.

Entirely disconnected from what was happening around her, Mum focused on the framed photographs of babies which lined every wall in the room, comparing them unfavourably to her own beautiful son, still sleeping soundly in her sister's arms. When the talking stopped and the disjointed words dropped from the air, a form appeared before her, and Mrs Jenner indicated where to sign.

Mum saw her hand reach out, lift the pen and scribble her signature on the proffered form, almost as though the hand belonged to someone else. Suddenly, she and Agnes were walking back through the gardens and, somewhere in her mind, Mum was aware that her sister's arms were deserted. She walked on obediently, her own arms empty, her heart frozen.

Many years later, Mum acknowledged in her writing that she must surely have known what was going on in that house when she saw the baby photos on the walls of the office. She later understood, although she had been well schooled throughout her life in locking down her emotions and functioning like an automaton, she should have asked questions before signing the form. She felt guilty for the remainder of her life, wondering how she could have been so coerced.

As they travelled home, neither of them spoke a word. When they opened the door to the flat, they saw their brother Don sitting at the kitchen table. He looked up expectantly; the beginning of a smile creasing his face. Taking in the empty arms of his sisters, his expression was instantly replaced by a puzzled look and a frown.

All was quiet for a moment as they stood frozen in the doorway, before Agnes broke the spell by bustling over to the sink to fill the kettle, saying *"It's the best thing for the baby, you know, as you'll have to get back to work as soon as you're well enough."*

Naturally, Mum had known she would need to pay her sister back for her board and keep since she had been living with her, and she also had a large hospital bill to pay. Nevertheless, she hadn't clearly considered what these expenses would mean, and was now faced with the painful, but inevitable truth.

Acid rising in her throat, she realised she had been floating around in a stupid dream, not tethered to reality at all. It was obvious now, without any financial support from Bryan's father, she couldn't hope to care for her son and provide his needs, unless she went back to work. With the crushing truth before her, she turned abruptly on her heel and walked to her room, closing the door quietly behind her.

She lay on the bed, hoping the tears clogging her throat would come and comfort her somehow but she couldn't weep. Her body was a yawning hollow cavern, and she buried herself in the blankets, filled with guilt and weakness. She could hear her brother and sister talking in the kitchen, their voices becoming a little heated from time to time, but she listened dispassionately until she fell asleep. She never discussed that terrible day with Don, only realising in later years her brother had been expecting her to arrive home with a new baby in her arms.

She hid herself away in her room for a week or so, either sleeping or staring blankly at the ceiling. Strangely, despite her despair, her body was regaining strength and when she felt strong enough, she helped around the house. She established something of a daily routine for herself, having learnt from years of experience that a strict routine could help her to cope with the unbearable.

Each day she stepped through the tasks one by one. She didn't think of anything beyond the task at hand and she counted the tasks off at day's end. Despite the spring sunshine beckoning through the windows, she didn't venture outdoors, craving to retreat permanently from the world.

As the days and nights of May slowly passed, the promise of sunshine on her face became too enticing, and one morning she asked Agnes for the shopping list. She offered to walk to the local shops and pick up the groceries they needed. After buying the few items on the list, she stepped out of the grocers with her string bag full, and, unthinkingly, turned left instead of right. Right was the way home, but she strolled the other way distractedly until she reached a tram stop.

On autopilot, she boarded a tram and sat down to stare straight ahead as the tram lumbered through Edinburgh's streets. The jolt as the tram left a stop caused an elderly man to bump into her as he passed. The bump woke her from her daze, and only then did she ask herself where on earth she was heading. She looked around in confusion, wondering anxiously where she was, feeling as if she had just woken from a dream.

As the tram jerked to a halt at the next stop, she peered out the window to get her bearings and saw a street which looked vaguely familiar to her. She jumped up and made it to the door just in time and scrambled down onto the pavement. After the tram rattled away in a cloud of dust, she looked both ways and realised she was standing on the street she had walked along with Agnes. It led to the house where she had left Bryan.

Rushing along the pavement, she came to the house she recognised and ran through the gate. It was only then she noticed many large high prams dotting the lawns, the babies having been placed outside for fresh air.

Desperately, she ran from one pram to another peering anxiously into each, knowing she would see Bryan in the next one, or the next. Her frantic search was in vain, even though every pram held one or two babies carefully tucked inside, she couldn't see Bryan among them. His little face had been stamped forever on her mind, and she knew that she would have known him.

Looking up in search of more prams, she saw a nurse in a starched white uniform marching hurriedly towards her.

She fled through the gate and back along the street to the tram stop. Hot, agonising, tears finally erupted from deep inside her as she stumbled aboard the tram and made her way home. She made no mention of her visit to her sister.

As she came bustling in through the door after work the following day, Agnes sent Billy to his room to read before quietly speaking to Mum, she was clearly furious. She said she had been embarrassed at work to be summoned to the telephone to receive a call from Mrs Jenner; staff were not supposed to receive personal calls. At the adoption centre, the nurse described the desperate looking intruder to her boss which had led to the call.

Agnes warned her angrily not to go back there again, *"You gave your baby up for adoption, don't you understand that?"* she shouted. Of course, Mum had heard Mrs Jenner's words on the dark day she had left her son behind, therefore she did know, but understanding what it meant had been buried deep within her for her own protection. She turned away from her angry sister and walked into her room; there were no words to describe the depth of her despair.

A letter arrived the following week with an appointment to go back to the centre. Once again, they sat before Mrs Jenner who told them a lovely, childless couple who lived in a beautiful home in the country, were adopting Bryan. They promised to love and cherish him always and give him the best education possible. With glowing references from respectable people within their community, Mrs Jenner assured them she was quite certain Bryan would have a wonderful life with them… etc… etc … the words went on.

Writing about this meeting forty years later, Mum acknowledges Mrs Jenner said more about the adoption but once again she had phased out. She had stared at the woman's moving mouth; the truth finally smashing into her heart and brain. Finally, it sank in: she would never see her little baby again. She writes, *"I had signed a form to say that I would turn my son over to strangers."* These words are darkly underlined on a page, smudged and blotched with her tears.

For the rest of her life, she struggled with dreadful guilt, wondering why she had listened to everyone who said it was impossible for her to keep Bryan. In her agony, she wondered if she could have found a way, if she had just tried harder, been less dumb, and the painful longing for her son never left her. She writes... *"the only thing I can think is, I gave him life, and I pray every night, that he is loved, and has happiness. And I would like to ask for his forgiveness, for giving him away, from me."*

On reading this, the dam I had built around my emotions finally collapses and I am brought to tears… my mother's attempt to find solace in the small mercy of giving her son life and her continued prayers for him are so powerful and heart-breaking! I cry for days, breaking down over the smallest thing. It may seem easy to judge her as weak for not fighting harder against '*giving*' her baby away to strangers. It was all but impossible for an unmarried woman to keep her baby in those times without at least the financial support of the father or her family. In so many ways, she was a naïve twenty-year-old girl, unaccustomed to making difficult decisions for herself, as complete obedience had been demanded of her throughout her life.

CHAPTER FOURTEEN

1947

When Mum's health had improved enough for her to go back to work, she trudged up to the telephone box and, taking a deep breath for courage, spoke to her old boss. After telling him she had recovered from her illness, she was relieved when he swiftly asked her to come back to her old position. On her first day back, she strode purposefully into the change room, a brave smile plastered on her face, despite the dancing butterflies in her stomach.

She nodded to a few of the other girls as she climbed into her uniform, and they nodded briefly back. It quickly became apparent however that her feelings of shame and guilt had created a wall between herself and the other girls, leading her to believe they all must know about the baby. Her dear friend Maisie had left the store by this time, having won a better position in Edinburgh's classiest store, and Mum felt isolated and uncomfortable.

She held her head up and set a façade firmly in place every day, trying to appear as the friendly, smiling assistant she had been before she left. However, over the following week, she became ever more certain that the girls were gossiping about her behind her back and judging her unkindly.

She felt that every time she entered the lunchroom, she was interrupting a group of girls who had been talking about her. How much of this perception was in her mind? She couldn't seem to break through the walls she had erected around herself. Unfortunately, her reserve led to the girls viewing her as being rather hoity-toity.

Thankfully, she was rescued before crumbling totally and leaving when a young woman named Annie returned from her annual holiday. She instantly broke through Mum's aloofness with her infectious, friendly personality, bringing Mum's guard down. Annie's vivacious prattle about film stars or fashion, or even the everyday grumbles about rations and the price of stockings, quickly brought the girls together. The atmosphere became more relaxed and friendly, leading to Mum's smile becoming more genuine as she stepped into the shop each morning. With her days now filled with work, she felt productive once again, returning home after her long days ready to help Agnes with the housework, eat and climb into bed.

Despite her weariness, she struggled to fall asleep. Sadness enveloped her when she was alone, and she lay in bed thinking of Bryan, wondering where he was and if he was being well cared for. Forcing herself to picture him in the arms of a strange woman, she prayed those arms were the loving, nurturing, kind of arms he would need as he grew up. As she cried herself to sleep each night, it was always difficult to drag herself out of bed in the morning. Though, once dressed and striding purposefully towards the tram stop, she would straighten her spine, lift her head, and get ready to face the day.

Over the next few months, she worked hard to clear the debts she owed to Agnes and the hospital. By browsing through the charity shops, especially those in the more affluent areas of Edinburgh, she slowly built a decent wardrobe for herself, buying a few good quality items which would last her for years.

Always an elegant dresser, she altered many of her purchases to fit in with the latest fashion by adding a touch of lace in just the right place or altering a neckline or hem. She remained the best charity shopper I ever knew and passed her skill in this department on to her children, grandchildren, and even great grandchildren. Her proficiency at making a dress suit her style was one she never lost.

When my brother Sandy dresses to go out, he dresses so well; quite snappy really. He has Mum's ability to piece an outfit together perfectly, no matter where it came from. My sister Cathy also has wonderful style, her carefully chosen, matching outfit putting me to shame when we go out together. Unfortunately, I didn't inherit Mum's wonderful fashion sense at all. I remember in the Sixties when jeans were not deemed to be proper attire for a self-respecting young lady, and she refused to buy them for me. I took on a babysitting job at fifteen and bought my own jeans, much to her dismay.

Even when we were adults and mothers ourselves, Mum would fuss around Cathy and I, tidying us up. I remember her leaning over a table or across a shopping aisle to push Cathy's fringe out of her eyes and smiling with satisfaction at the result. I think she just gave up on me with a sigh eventually.

***

When her debt was finally paid off, a strange weather pattern brought an Indian summer to Scotland, promising to last for at least a couple of days and Annie suggested she and Mum go for a little break to the seaside. They had a fantastic time; with the weather so unseasonably warm, they walked arm in arm down to the beach daily to work on their tans. They wore cotton dresses and warm cardigans over their new Rita Hayworth style swimsuits.

Annie never questioned Mum about her long absence from work, leaving her to relax and enjoy each precious moment, The feeling of freedom was overwhelming at times. They strolled along the esplanade both nights, eating fish and chips, giggling like little girls and generally enjoying themselves. Over those precious few days, Mum's health improved, as did her outlook, and they both travelled home with rosy cheeks and happy smiles.

A few weeks after the little holiday, Don popped into the flat one blustery evening. November had begun wreaking its vengeance for the short sun-filled days the autumn had delivered only weeks ago. As he sat at the table, cuppa in hand, he broke the news that Bessie and their father wanted her to come home. Don was living at home again after being demobilised (demobbed) from the forces, and he said he missed her so much; the house was too quiet without her. Mum was astounded!

After everything that had happened in that house, why did anyone think she would go back? As she lay in bed that night, she thought it through and realised it was obvious that Bessie wanted her back to be a scullery maid again. But she was deeply suspicious of her father's motive. *"I'm not going back to that house,"* she said to herself, *"I'm fine here, I'm working, paying my way, and helping Agnes, why on earth would I go there?"* In her mind, that was the end of it!

At breakfast a few days later, she told Agnes about Don's visit and the request to come home. Her sister was quiet for a moment, holding her tea between her hands for warmth and sipping thoughtfully, before saying *"Well Sheila, I wasn't going to broach this until the weekend, but George and I will be marrying in a month's time."* She continued *"Billy and I will move into George's home straight after the wedding, and I'm sorry but there are no spare rooms in his house."*

Stunned, Mum felt as though the scaffolding which had been holding her together since the news of her pregnancy was disintegrating around her, leaving her weak and vulnerable again. She understood that she couldn't afford to keep the flat by herself. Speechlessly, she walked into her room to dress and left for work in shocked silence.

That night, as she lay on her bed thinking, tears running down into her hair, she questioned everything that had happened to her and wondered what she had done to deserve it. She wasn't angry with Agnes, either for her part in Bryan's adoption or for marrying such a good man, but she realised living with her sister had provided her with safety, peace, and a security she had never known before.

Agnes had always taken control of every situation in the family. To be fair, her sister had taken her in and arranged what she honestly believed to be the best thing. Over the past months, Mum had been slowly but steadily clambering out of a dark hole, but now it was as if the hole was about to draw her back into its brutal vortex. What was she to do?

In the end she could see no other way out of her situation and, as soon as her sister's lovely wedding was over, she dragged her feet slowly back through the front door of the house on Easter Road, suitcase in hand, heart heavy. Later in life, she looked back and wondered why she didn't search for other options at the time. Perhaps she could have found board with someone, as Margaret had done, or tried to rent a flat to share with some of the girls in the shop.

Through the lens of hindsight, she began to understand that her sister's wedding and natural move into George's home, leaving her essentially homeless, had occurred on the heels of losing Bryan and the shock of it all had hurtled her back into her compliant self. She felt the old familiar sensation of entering a dark cave when she entered the house for the first time since leaving with Agnes. She realised that she was afraid of lapsing back into the timid, obedient and vulnerable girl she had been.

***

After settling back into her room, Mum popped into the kitchen and started working. She was thankful to discover within the first week or two that living there was a fraction easier than it had been before she left. There was only one boarder in the house now as the others had moved home, the servicemen having returned to the positions they held before the war.

This meant her household chores were easier, taking up much less of her time. She was surprised to find her stepmother was also a little less brusque with her than beforehand and, most importantly, she rarely saw her father at all.

Not long after her return, she popped into the corner shop when she finished work one day to see the warm-hearted Mrs McAllister. The woman was so glad to see her that she took her into her arms, hugging her tightly. After holding her back at arm's length to look her over, she exclaimed how she was relieved to see her looking well. She quietly warned Mum that Bessie had told the neighbours the whole family had been devastated about her condition, going on to say they didn't know who the baby's father was.

The intimation was it could have been any one of the lads from the services. Seeing Mum's eyes fill with tears, she sympathetically advised her not to upset herself about it and to let it go, saying no one really believed Bessie, knowing what she was like.

As she walked home, Mum mused… "How typical of Bessie to make herself out as a victim. After all, she had practically begged Mum to go out with Tommy again to get her bedside table finished." Coming to a decision, she lifted her chin and firmly put her stepmother's treachery behind her so that she could maintain the reasonable peace which now existed between them.

With Mum's decision to move forward with her life, she decided to return to the dance halls. She still loved to dance, with the music taking hold of her, she could forget her pain and dancing was again the highlight of her life. She went to the dance halls with her girlfriends on the two nights she was permitted to go out, Wednesdays and Saturdays. She still had to keep to her curfew, and she always refused the request of any fellow who wanted to walk her home.

She was excited when Don arrived home from work one Friday night and asked if she would go to the dance with him. He was given free rein to come and go as he wanted. Due to it being Don's idea, Bessie gave her permission and Mum quickly changed into her 'glad rags' and dancing shoes, breathless with anticipation.

As she entered the hall, her arm linked with her tall, handsome big brother's, she felt rather proud. Dressed in his best suit, Don made a striking partner, his film star looks matching her own, however as soon as he swept her onto the dance floor, she was dismayed to find he had 'two left feet.' Her toes were soon throbbing from being trodden on and she swiftly became dizzy from his constant need to whirl her around and around, so she decided to sit the next dance out. She plonked herself down and sat, fanning her red face, while she surveyed the room.

She soon spied a lovely friend named Betty, chatting to a group of girls at the other end of the hall, sparkling and laughing as usual. Mum suggested to Don that he ask her to dance. As soon as they walked onto the dance floor together, she could see they complemented one another and as they waltzed around the room, they were soon talking and laughing comfortably together. It wasn't long before they were courting, and within a year, the wedding bells rang; she was ecstatic for them both. They made such a handsome couple, and she was happy her role as Cupid had worked out so well.

CHAPTER FIFTEEN

1948

It was a cold, dismal evening in late December of 1947 with bitter winds blowing straight off the North Sea and ugly, grey slush heaped by the roadsides. Winter already felt endless. Mum sat on a tram at the end of a long day, rubbing her gloved hands together for warmth as she headed home. She listened vaguely to the dreary conversations around her, everyone moaning about the weather and rationing, and she realised it was time to shake herself and make a move to improve her life.

Using this time to think, she devised a plan. Although there were no advertised positions currently available in the shop where Maisie worked, she would write to the store manager and apply there, outlining her extensive experience as a shoe fitter. Her friend was enjoying her position and had urged Mum to apply. The store paid their staff well and enjoyed a high reputation for excellence in customer service and high-quality products.

J and R Allen was a large department store with a sizable shoe department which only stocked shoes of the highest quality. The management and staff were proud of its custom cobbling department, where handmade bespoke shoes were crafted for their most valued customers, including the royal family. After mailing the carefully written application letter she waited anxiously, fingers crossed, to hear back. Two weeks later, she was invited to attend an interview, and hardly believing her luck, she searched through her wardrobe, deciding what to wear.

On the morning of the interview, she dressed in her freshly-pressed suit which matched beautifully with the peep-toed shoes she had shone to within an inch of their life the night before. Shaking in those shiny shoes, she entered the manager's plush office at the appointed time and, once seated, used her best voice to answer his questions. He grilled her about her previous knowledge and experience and asked for her viewpoint on customer service. Towards the end of the gruelling interview, she felt concerned that she may not have answered his probing questions as well as she could have. Her nerves having gotten the better of her a little.

As the interview was reaching the end, the manager's last question was to ask why she wanted to work in his store. Sucking in a deep breath, she sat bolt upright, tilted her head back a little and looked him directly in the eye. *"I want to better myself, sir, and this is just the place to do it"* she said boldly. As she stood to go, she noticed a slight smile trying to escape his lips as she shook his proffered hand and left the office, head high! Trembling but triumphant, she felt that she had done the best she could, and her hard-won confidence and determination had shone through. She started her new job a month later.

She blossomed in her new role and the added bonus of working with her dear friend Maisie again was the icing on the cake. Her ability to develop rapport quickly with customers, especially children, was soon noticed. They would sit quietly for her as she spoke softly with them, making them laugh and they never grumbled and squirmed while she measured their feet.

Specialised training was soon offered to her, and she was eager to learn the complexities of measuring for people who suffered from disabilities such as clubfoot. She would take careful measurements, spend time with the customer, helping them to choose a design and order the shoes from the custom department.

Her self-assurance grew the more she believed in herself. Of course, nothing had changed at home and, as she entered the door nightly, she became the other version of herself, a quiet, obedient woman with downcast eyes.

***

She began to casually date a young man named James, a quiet, deep-thinking fellow who always treated her with respect, being a perfect gentleman. Her brother-in-law, George, had introduced them one night at dinner and over the next week or two often spoke highly of him. James was a gentle and rather unassuming young man who lived with his widowed mother.

As a young lawyer with a promising future ahead of him, George thought they would be perfect together. She was invited by James's mother to share a simple lunch with them every Sunday and they developed a mutual regard for one another. She really liked Mum and it wasn't long before she was dropping hints about the couple's future. Both James and Mum however were in no rush, happy with the way things were. They were enjoying each other's company and were not ready for any pressure, their relationship was almost platonic.

James enjoyed a quiet life when he wasn't working hard and didn't like dancing much or attending the cinema, so she still went by herself on occasion. Eventually, James succumbed to pressure, asking her to marry him. She gently refused his offer. The fact that he really didn't like dancing was perhaps a factor in her decision.

The late spring sunshine finally made its anaemic appearance through the lunchroom window at work one day. A few of the girls, including Maisie and Mum, were perched at the only table which offered them some precious sunshine. As they chatted, Maisie mentioned a young man named Alex with whom she had become friends.

***

After coming home from his time fighting in the navy, he had taken a job working in the shoemaking department of the store. She laughingly said Alex had been pestering her to ask her friend Sheila to go out on a date with him. Smiling at the thought, Mum rather flippantly said she wasn't interested. Maisie, however, asked her again and again over the next couple of days until frustratedly, Mum said *"Why, can't he just ask me himself if he's so keen?"* Maisie explained that although Alex was a lovely man, he was very shy and was betting on her vouching for him, wearing Mum down until she agreed on a date. She tossed her head, saying *"For the very last time, I'm not interested!"*

A few weeks later, the sun finally shone warmly from a clear blue sky making the city's stone buildings sparkle. The famous Princes Street gardens, across the road from the store, burst forth with an amazing array of spring flowers and beckoned everyone outdoors. At morning tea, Maisie took Mum's arm firmly and suggested a walk there during lunch hour and later they found a spot in the sun to enjoy their sandwiches.

After eating, they strolled along the heavily-scented path, admiring the floral displays until they were approached by a young man who stopped before them, red faced and stammering *"Oh hello Maisie."* Maisie introduced him to Mum as her dear friend Alex, and they shook hands; his grip was firm but a little rough and callused. His shy smile, sparkling green eyes and thick mop of curly, ginger-blond hair intrigued her immediately. The three of them walked companionably along the pathways between the garden beds, enjoying the sunshine and flowers and chatting about the dark turn of events in Europe.

As they discussed current affairs, including the looming danger of a cold war between Russia and the USA, she was impressed by his obvious intelligence and sense of humour. When they parted, Alex invited her to come to the pictures with him that weekend and she surprised herself by happily saying 'Yes.' As they climbed the stairs to their floor afterwards,

Maisie mischievously said, *"I told you he was lovely and yes, bumping into him wasn't an accident."*

Over the next month, Alex and Mum enjoyed each other's company and met regularly, keeping the relationship friendly and casual as they got to know each other. She found being in his company made her feel safe and peaceful; and she especially enjoyed his sense of humour and calm mannerisms. When he told her he had first fallen for her because of her ears, she was taken aback, expecting a romantic remark and asked, *"What's wrong with them"*? Trying to retrieve the situation he quickly told her he had been sitting in the lunchroom, minding his own business, and chomping on his scotch pie when he first saw her.

She had come bustling in through the staffroom door and headed straight for the large, black kettle which usually sat on the lowered flame gently gurgling away. He watched her as she picked up the heavy kettle and banged it angrily under the tap to fill, all the while grumbling to herself, *"You'd think they could at least fill it up and put it back on the boil; no consideration for others!"* Still muttering under her breath, she had dashed around making preparations for her cuppa and took her sandwich from its brown paper bag then stood, waiting impatiently for the kettle to boil, toes tapping.

While all this fuss was going on, her tiny, shell-like, ears had become increasingly red until they were positively glowing with indignation. He became mesmerised by them and watched her surreptitiously when she eventually sat down to eat, still huffing and puffing angrily. He knew he had to meet her somehow but, being shy, he couldn't bring himself to approach her. She seemed quite formidable, and he felt she was much too beautiful for him. In today's parlance, we would say he felt rather as though he was 'punching above his weight.'

A month or two passed with Mum seeing Alex on a regular basis. They went to the cinema and dance halls dancing well together. Strolling in the park on the long summer evenings, talking about world events, was enjoyable and they always ended the night with laughter when he spun a tale or two.

Alex at once realised she was 'the one'! One evening, after meandering through the Kings Park, near Holyrood, he invited her up to the family flat for a cuppa. His family lived in Parkside Street, only a short walk from the park, and as they strolled along the cobbled streets, Mum grew increasingly nervous. She was about to meet his parents. When they came to a dark stone tenement Alex opened a green door which led straight into a stairwell and she noticed both the door and the stairwell, unlike so many in the city, were sparkling clean.

When Alex ushered her through the door on the left of the first-floor landing, a woman looked up from where she was sitting by the old black range, obviously surprised! She smiled fleetingly but was evidently rather flustered, at once standing and bustling around nervously. As she crossed the room, she scolded Alex lightly saying, *"Och son, you should have let me know you were bringing a lassie home."*

Whisking the newspaper off the table and replacing it with a snow-white linen cloth, she proceeded to lay four, fragile looking china cups and saucers out for tea. In the middle of the table, she placed a large teapot along with a cut glass milk jug and sugar bowl.

As she served the tea, Mum observed Alex's mother and liked what she saw. Mrs Morrison was short and a little stout, with a ready smile, curly grey hair and a pinny clamped around her ample waist. Mum would later learn she almost lived in a pinny which she would whisk off only when leaving the house. She shook Mum's hand warmly, saying *"Just call us Granny and Pop pet, like everyone else."*

His father was sitting by the fire with a newspaper open on his lap and, after standing to greet her with a shy smile and sincere handshake, he quietly sat back down, returning to his paper. Short and slightly built, he somehow exuded hidden strength; one would call him 'wiry.' His almost bald head was barely covered by a thin, grey 'comb over' and his green eyes, so like his son's, sparkled.

Although the room they were sitting in was small and cramped, every inch of it shone. The main room served as a bedroom, with a double bed set into a curtained alcove, a kitchen/dining room and a sitting room. There was also a small double bedroom, a tiny box room, and an inside toilet so Alex's tour of the house was over as the tea finished brewing in the cosy-covered teapot.

After enjoying their tea, they stayed to chat for a while and a bubbly young woman rushed in through the front door enthusiastically. She helped herself to a cuppa and with a warm smile, took Mum's hand saying she was Alex's wonderful big sister, Jeanie. She turned towards Pop then and made a cheeky remark to him, shocking Mum.

The old man swiftly launched himself out of his chair and chased her round the room, but she laughingly dodged around the crowded room, keeping out of his way. After a minute, they stopped running and, puffing and red faced, they bent over and cackled like hens. Catching their breath, they sat down companionably next to the fire and Mum looked at them both in total astonishment. It was easy to see what this family lacked in material wealth, they more than made up for in plain, down-to-earth goodness.

She was later to discover the family had suffered many hardships in the past, beginning in World War One. Pop was a Corporal in the Queen's Cameron Highlanders and was labelled as 'Missing in Action" for almost seven years. Injured in France in 1915, he was captured by the Germans and taken to a prisoner of war camp. For some reason, he was still missing when the war ended and surprised Granny by arriving home shortly after Hogmany, 1921.

He may have told his patient wife why he didn't return earlier but the rest of the family never knew. Perhaps his time in the trenches and the prisoner of war camp had affected him mentally, or maybe he wandered around when the camp had been liberated, not knowing where he was or how to get home.

While he was away, Granny struggled to manage on a meagre war pension. She supplemented the allowance by taking in rich people's washing. Every day, she would collect their laundry in an old pram and wheel it for a mile or so to the 'steamy,' a communal laundry equipped with iron tubs, boilers, steam driven spinning tubs, drying chambers and steam irons. This backbreaking work was the only way she could pay the rent and feed her three young children, Mary, Ina and John.

When Pop finally returned from the war, they somehow moved on with their married life and promptly added another four children to their brood. First came Jeanie, followed swiftly by Kenneth, Alex, and, finally, George. Of the many hardships they had endured, and overcome, none was as profound as the loss they suffered when their eldest son, John, died.

He had been killed when a German submarine attacked his ship during the Second World War, scuppering it to the bottom of the sea. Their pain and loss never spoiled their characteristic quiet, no-nonsense and determined natures. Mum told me that one of Granny's favourite sayings was, *"God will always gie ye the back to bear the burden."*

Mum soon felt quite at home, all nervousness banished in the warm, informal atmosphere surrounding the family. She was entranced by the lovely example of family life she came to know and realised it was what she wanted for her own family one day.

***

One Saturday night, as they left the Palais, Alex asked her to come with him to see a movie on Tuesday night. This was one of the evenings she wasn't allowed out and she had to explain she was only free two nights a week. He found this shocking… *"You're twenty-four years old, why can't you go out when you want to hen?"* he blustered in astonishment.

She told him life wasn't so simple for her because of her father's rules. She went on to explain that she also had so many chores to do each week and Tuesday nights were taken up with starching and ironing. He asked if he could come to the house to keep her company as she worked so she received permission from Bessie. She wasn't too worried about her father, as he was absent from home most weeknights. If he did stay at home, he was generally unseen, spending the evening in the parlour, listening to music on the wireless and reading.

When Tuesday night arrived, Alex sat comfortably beside the kitchen fire reading his newspaper while she got on with the ironing. As she worked, he kept her amused with his spin on some of the articles he was reading, even impersonating the BBC newsreader reporting the news that Princess Elizabeth and her husband Phillip were expecting a baby.

In fits of giggles at his silly voice, she looked up when the kitchen door opened, expecting to see Bessie, but was aghast to see her father walk towards the pantry. He didn't seem to notice either of them as he walked past. Carefully placing the iron down, she took a deep breath and walked towards him, saying *"Father, I'd like you to meet Alex Morrison."* Alex stood with a ready smile and an extended hand, expecting her father to grasp it. Instead of reaching his hand out in return, his eyes roamed all around the room, ignoring Alex completely.

Time seemed to stand still as they stood there in a sort of Mexican standoff with Alex's face gradually becoming bright red, before her father finally was forced to look at him and take his hand in a limp grip. Her father didn't say a word, or offer a smile while shaking hands, but quickly dropped his hand as though scalded and stalked out of the room.

As can be imagined, Alex was deeply embarrassed, and Mum could see he was awfully angry. He sat down in the chair without saying anything about what had happened, and they chatted on companionably for another hour or so.

When it was time for Alex to leave, they stood in the hallway to say goodnight and slowly Alex leaned towards her and placed his hand gently behind her neck before kissing her tenderly. She found herself leaning into his warm, gentle kiss and, when they broke apart, he whispered that he loved her very, very much. She didn't know what to say; she had certainly enjoyed his kiss and loved spending time with him but was afraid to let herself trust that anyone would be able to truly love her.

During the following month, Alex told Mum he loved her dearly often enough to create cracks in her shell. She took the risk of believing him, despite being aware they came from such different worlds. Alex saw himself as a strictly working-class man. Even their manner of speaking was different. Mum had been raised to speak 'The Queen's English' and despite his intelligence, Alex often used words which revealed his upbringing in the tenements.

As their friendship deepened, they talked about their childhoods, discussed their dreams for the future and also the people they had previously dated. Alex's tales of growing up were filled with laughter, friends and family. There were so many good stories even though the family had often gone hungry during the depression, when Pop couldn't find work.

Good friends were very important to Alex, leading him to declining a full scholarship to a prestigious grammar school.

Alex said he was happy at the local school with his friends, telling his teachers he couldn't accept the offer as his mother couldn't afford the uniforms. He had become engaged to his childhood sweetheart while on leave from the navy, but his heart had been broken when he discovered his fiancée had been seeing other men while he was away.

In turn, Mum told him about her relationship with James, which she had ended months ago, much to his mother's dismay. She also shared a little of her violent childhood, telling him about some of the cruelty her father had inflicted on most of his children. However, her deep shame wouldn't allow her to share the repulsive secret of what had happened to her younger self in her father's bed on those dark Sundays.

***

With the deepening of their friendship, there was no doubt in Alex's mind that he wanted to marry this beautiful, strong, fragile woman so he eventually plucked up enough courage to propose. They were standing on a tram at the time, each gripping a leather strap which hung from the ceiling, when he leaned close to her ear and asked her to be his wife.

She was so taken aback by his proposal she didn't know what to say, she had come to feel something for him which she thought might be love but knew she couldn't possibly marry him without disclosing that she had a son. To buy some time to think, she promised to meet him after work the following day.

Tentatively entering their favourite café, knees and hands shaking, Mum sat opposite him at a quiet corner table and, taking a deep, deep breath, she exposed her painful secret, leaving nothing out. Her shame at the rape, her pregnancy, Bryan's birth and his adoption, all came tumbling out. Her head was lowered the whole time, eyes glued to the wooden tabletop where her tears dripped, unheeded.

Alex sat quietly giving her space to talk and holding her trembling hand across the table as she unburdened herself. When she finished, she dared to raise her tear-streaked face to his, expecting to see disgust or revulsion. What she did see was a mixture of horror and compassion, and he leaned over the table to kiss her lips gently. He thanked her for telling the truth and said, '*I still love you hen, it wasn't your fault!*'

He went on to say they wouldn't speak of the rape, or Bryan again, leaving it all behind them when they married. Although relieved he still wanted her to be his wife, she was adamant that he must take time to think about what she had told him before she would answer his proposal. He reluctantly agreed they wouldn't see one another for a while, and they set a date to meet back in the café three weeks later.

Three mornings later, Alex climbed the stairs to the sales floor and desperately grabbed her by the hand. They slipped into the stockroom, where he whispered that he couldn't wait any longer; there was no way he could be any surer of his love. She was taken aback by his fervour and agreed to meet him for lunch.

They clasped hands across the table, and Alex proposed again. This time, with tears welling in her eyes, she answered with a timid, unsure *"Yes."* Over the moon, they talked of their future, and he repeated his belief that every word she had told him about the rape was true. Once again, he said it would be best if they moved on from the horror with a clean slate and would never mention any of it again. She believed the person sitting opposite was a real man, the kind of man who would never knowingly hurt her and she trusted him with her damaged heart.

She sensed in him a strength below the surface of his peaceful exterior and felt sure she could trust him completely. They decided there was no reason to wait so they posted their Banns immediately. Until 1978, the Banns, which were a notice of intention to marry, were legally required to be read out in the church one month before a wedding, thus ensuring enough time for any objections to be raised. (This is no longer a legal requirement in the UK.)

Alex's announcement that the assault and birth of her son wouldn't be raised ever again must have felt like a relief to her and I'm sure it was well meant. However, the unintentional outcome was that the store of potent secrets from her past remained under lock and key for years. Without light and air, the secrets festered and gnawed inside her mind, causing terrible periods of black depression which lasted for weeks or on one occasion, months.

They married on Christmas Eve 1946 in the little church where Alex's parents had been married. Mum wore a gorgeous, petrol blue suit with a spray of flowers pinned to the lapel, a matching hat, and suede, peep-toe heels. Alex wore the double-breasted, pin striped 'demob' suit which he received when he was released from the navy. All servicemen received a full three-piece suit, along with a shirt, hat and shoes, when they were 'demobbed' to help them settle into life at home. This also boosted income for textile manufacturers and tailors as they made the adjustment from making uniforms.

The flower in his lapel was a carnation, her favourite flower. When she nervously arrived at church just before the service, she noticed that she wasn't the only anxious one, Alex looked really quite unwell. His complexion, quite pale at the best of times, was totally grey and even the wide smile which creased his face when he spotted her did nothing to add any colour. She discovered later he had been unable to sleep the night before the wedding due to his nerves and had spent the majority of the wee hours on the toilet.

It had been six months to the day since their meeting in Princes street gardens. Mum's bridesmaid was her dear friend Maisie who had orchestrated the 'chance' meeting and Alex's best man was his younger brother, George. As it was a Friday, they had only five guests. After the brief ceremony, they trotted along in a happy group to the flat for tea, sandwiches, granny's homemade wedding cake and a wee nip of whisky for the toast.

There was no offer to pay anything towards the wedding costs from her father; he didn't give them a gift or offer his congratulations. In fact, he ignored the entire event. He had paid for and hosted a wedding breakfast for Don and Betty in the parlour only a month earlier. When she walked out of his house on the day of her wedding, wielding her small suitcase in one hand and her wedding suit in the other, her heart lifted, knowing she would never have to go back there again.

***

When the refreshments were eaten and the wedding toast made, the blissfully happy couple boarded a bus to Callander, a small village about an hour from the city, for a weekend honeymoon. When they skipped down from the bus, hand in hand, the snow was falling heavily. Mum was still wearing her peep-toed, suede high heels, and within seconds her feet were wet and icy cold.

Every so often, as they made their way across the park towards their tiny hotel, Alex stopped to crouch down, take one of her feet in his hands and rub the circulation back into it. She often spoke about his kindness that day and said it was one of the loveliest things she had ever felt; she had never known that type of gentle, caring love existed.

Once they reached the road, they skipped along, trying not to fall in the snow, while singing *"We're off to see the wizard, the wonderful Wizard of Oz"* and attempting to keep themselves from freezing. The future beckoned them forward, as bright as the newly fallen snow, sparkling with possibilities as yet unknown.

They spent a wonderful few days in Callander getting to know each other better, going for walks, talking, and enjoying the full Scottish breakfast they were served each morning. I remember Mum laughingly telling me about another honeymoon couple who were staying in the hotel. When asked if they minded sharing a table with the other couple, they had happily agreed, thinking it would be fun to share stories.

As it turned out, at every meal, the couple were seen with books open in front of them, reading. After the initial greeting, they wouldn't speak for the rest of the meal. At the first meal, Alex whispered to her that he could think of much better ways to spend his honeymoon than reading. They spent the rest of the meal trying to hold their laughter under control but fell into their room afterwards, giggling like silly children.

CHAPTER SIXTEEN

1949 – 1951

Travelling home from their short honeymoon, the happy newlyweds were astonished to discover how much money they had left. Between them, they scraped together only four pence, not much to rely on until payday. They weren't too worried though, agreeing their short honeymoon had been worth every penny, they knew they would manage.

As they burst through the door of the flat, laughing together, Granny and Pop shared a knowing glance and a smile, glad to see their son so happy. The couple quickly settled into the flat's one bedroom. There was a severe housing shortage across the country at the end of the war and families were seizing whatever housing they could get. As they settled into their new lives, Mum soon realised that her instinct had been right in trusting Alex with her future.

He was gentle and patient, especially as she struggled in the bedroom department, where sometimes feelings of fear and dread would engulf her out of the blue, leaving her shaking and crying even when they both wanted to make love. She wanted to be relaxed with him in bed, and there were many times when she was angry with herself for breaking down. His tenderness was endless, and he never became angry with her. Over time she learned how to let go a little, most of the time anyway.

***

Alex's childhood home was a haven for the newlyweds and Mum soon came to admire and respect Granny immensely. Never one for idle chit-chat or gossip, she didn't appear to have a bad word for anyone; and didn't see the point in poking her nose into other people's nonsense. She had known enough hardship in her own life.

Saturday nights were crazy in the flat. All Alex's siblings and their families would cram inside; the women cooking tea and the men huddled before the fire doing their football pools. After everyone was fed, the table would be pulled into the middle of the room and everyone sat down to play cards, laughing and talking ten to the dozen.

Mum loved being part of this large, warm family. It was as though they had reached their arms out to encircle her and take her in as one of their own. She and George's wife Mary, both newcomers to the family, soon developed a friendship, their shared experience bringing them close.

***

Within a year of their marriage, Mum was ecstatic to discover she was pregnant. Her excitement was so hard to contain that she burst through the door breathlessly after her doctor's appointment, blurting the wonderful news out to Granny without meaning to, and collapsing into fits of giggles. She felt bad about not keeping it secret until her man came home but he was as happy as Larry when she told him and twirled her around the room in a dizzying waltz.

As money was in terribly short supply, Mum planned to keep working as long as possible before the birth. However, she was told in no uncertain terms she was risking her own life and that of her unborn child if she kept working. Dismayed, she told Granny how frustrated she was about her health once again interfering with her plans. When she declared that she was going to keep working a bit longer, Granny, ever the voice of reason, challenged her, "*What if something happens to the wee one because of your stubbornness,*" She said, "*You willnae forgive yersel lass.*" Alex of course, agreed, he didn't like Mum working anyway, and she handed in her notice the following week.

***

My big brother was born on 7 July 1950, to the delight of everyone in the family and who, in the tradition of the times, was named for his father, Alexander Taylor Morrison… shortened to Sandy. While Mum was in hospital for the regulation two weeks after the birth, Alex visited her nightly. While on the bus, he wrote funny little letters, romantic notes, or poems to her, slipping them under her pillow when he left.

When the ward was shushed for the night, she would huddle down into the starched white sheets and read his latest offering, sometimes suppressing an embarrassed giggle at a risqué word or two. Mum bound those letters in ribbon and kept them all her life.

Recently Cathy and I came across this bundle of letters while searching for photographs. Feeling naughty, we read a few of them and giggled to see they had little jokes between them in regard to their sex life. Then we wiped tears from our eyes on reading his beautiful, tender words, reassuring her of the depths of his love. In these letters, he calls her his precious angel.

When Alex arrived to collect Mum from the hospital, she was surprised to see his chest was about to burst through his jacket and he proudly carried Sandy in his arms, clutching him tightly as the bus wound its way through the city streets. His dream of a wee family had begun.

Granny was a great help to Mum in the early days as she settled into motherhood, although Mum discovered that some of her baby care tips were terribly old fashioned. At Sandy's first nappy change when they were home, Granny placed a needle and thread, two cardboard milk bottle tops, a penny and a bandage on the table for her. When Mum asked her what they were for, Granny showed her how to sew a binder on to keep his belly button in. The penny was placed between the two milk tops and put firmly against his navel, then the bandage was sewn into place to hold it there. This was to be done at every single nappy change until his navel had fully healed.

To Mum's relief, Margaret told her not to bother with that old-fashioned nonsense, adding that Sandy's navel would be fine without it. Mum changed him in the bedroom after this incident, not wanting to hurt Granny's feelings and she and Mary felt a little ashamed as they giggled about it later.

Most of the tips Granny offered were received gratefully, as Mum had no experience in caring for a tiny, fragile baby. She would pick him up as soon as he made one little whimper and took him into the bed at night when he wouldn't settle in his cane washing basket. Granny warned her, *"You'll be makin' a rod for your own back if you let him rule you lass"* but Mum felt it was the right thing to do, she couldn't bear to hear him cry.

Alex wasn't happy sharing the bed with a squirming little one and bought him a dummy, which Sandy promptly and utterly rejected. Many sleepless nights followed before, in desperation, Alex followed his friend's advice to *"Just rub a wee bit of Scotch on his gums, to settle him."* Well, this only made Sandy worse and, in the end, Mum's tears and Alex's exhaustion won. Sandy slept in their bed until he was a toddler, and Mum often said that that she knew she had been overprotective in those days.

During those early struggles with motherhood, Mum also endured many battles with chronic, debilitating bronchitis, and soon lost the little weight she had gained during pregnancy until her clothes were hanging loosely on her thin frame. The local GP advised a move from the area as the air there wasn't good for her health. The tenement building sat directly across the road from a coal yard which sent coal dust flying into the air all day long, and the Holyrood brewery was around the corner, belching smoke and fermenting odours into the air six days a week.

Alex was annoyed with the doctor, feeling that he was putting the family down and argued with Mum saying, *"This place was good enough when I was a boy. Who the hell does he think he is"*? Thankfully, Granny's wisdom came to the fore, and she reminded him that Mum's precarious health and Sandy's persistent cough were more important than his pride. They began searching for somewhere else to live.

Finding somewhere to live was no mean task in a city bursting at the seams with returned servicemen and their fast-growing families. Building had effectively come to a halt since 1914, with the hard years of the Great Depression sandwiched between two world wars causing a shortage of manpower and money. Men who were not enlisted in the services had been directed into essential war industries such as ammunition factories or farms.

As the country frantically rushed to rebuild after World War Two ended, domestic housing was at the lower end of a long list of construction projects. Despite the lack of adequate housing for families, an unprecedented number of babies were being born across the country, not surprising with servicemen returning to their former lives. The baby boomer generation had arrived; a generation which would later become the agents of unprecedented social change.

Shortly after Sandy's first birthday, Mum and Alex were ecstatic to find they were expecting another baby. When they shared their good news with the rest of the family, Mary also said she was expecting, and they both were thrilled to know they would have their babies around the same time. It was now imperative to find a new place for the growing family to live, and they became quite desperate.

Luckily, Mum's brother Don, had found a slightly larger flat for himself, his wife and their baby daughter, meaning the two roomed flat they had been renting right in the centre of Leith was about to become available. They took over the lease of the corner flat, excited to have their own space at last.

Unfortunately, they soon discovered there were many problems, such as having only a single ring kerosene stove for cooking, no bathroom, and a toilet which they had to climb down one floor to access. The toilet was shared between three other flats and tended to be cold and smelly.

Adding to these troubles, Mum noticed Sandy had a persistent rash around his pyjama collar every morning and after trying different creams, she took him to the doctor. He took one look and declared that they looked like bites, "*Probably just bed bugs*" he said. Horrified, Mum went to see Granny who said all the old tenements had bed bugs in the walls as the many layers of wallpaper, with new paper plastered over the old, created crevices for them to live in.

She suggested a visit to the health department to get the flat fumigated and they moved back in with Granny and Pop for a couple of weeks to avoid being contaminated by the disinfection chemicals. Granny had told Mum many tenants were too ashamed to get the fumigators in, preferring bed bugs to the shame of neighbours thinking they were dirty. Mum couldn't believe the craziness of this attitude.

When the cold of autumn crept in, they struggled to heat the flat with the open fire as the chimney constantly belched smoke back into the room. Despite many complaints to the landlord, it was not fixed. This meant opening the two windows in the flat every now and again to let the smoke blow through. One day Mum lit the fire in the morning and by lunchtime was forced to open the windows. Within ten minutes, she was startled by a loud, insistent knock on the door and, opening it, was shocked by a police officer rushing right past her.

Once inside the flat, he looked frantically around, expecting to see the place on fire and she explained the problem with the chimney. He had been directing traffic on the busy intersection below when he had seen the smoke billowing from the window, and she told him the landlord wouldn't fix it. He became angry, saying the landlord was being derelict in his duty, and promised to help. Two days later, the problem was taken care of by a man going up onto the roof and replacing the broken 'granny' on top of the chimney.

***

Alex's job paid very little, and they struggled financially. At times like these, Alex would often come out with a well-known Scots saying, *"Don't worry hen, we haven't died a winter yet."* His attempt to reassure her that all would be well would just make her grit her teeth in frustration at his optimism.

He started a new job as an insurance premium collector as he was convinced the pay would be far better than his previous work when the commissions came pouring in. The position required him to go and visit people who had taken out life insurance policies to collect their premiums once a month. Unfortunately, he was hopeless in this job, as he often felt sorry for the housewives who would say they didn't have the money. There were excuses galore; husbands who hadn't given them the money, husbands who were laid off, or drunken husbands.

As he was only paid a monthly retainer, relying on commissions to make a decent wage, his pay was often terrible. The promise of earning enough to get them into a better flat was a long way off. I know this could make him sound weak but in fact he had a strong character and could be very stubborn. In some ways, his downfall was his kind-heartedness. He would 'go the extra mile' to help others; he couldn't bear to see people or animals suffer.

CHAPTER SEVENTEEN

1952

Despite the dire housing situation and money worries, the little family were soon thrilled at the prospect of a new baby and Mum's belly was quickly obvious on her thin frame. When the cold set in with a vengeance in autumn, she developed a chronic cough which kept her awake at night, leading her to drag herself, exhausted, through each day. She struggled to care for Sandy, cook and clean. She also had to hand wash their clothing and trudge down to the washhouse with the linens when they piled up.

A visit to the washhouse meant bundling the dirty towels and linen into the pram with Sandy. She would carefully lug the pram down the stairs and navigate the long walk there and back in the biting wind and haul the pram back up the stairs at the end of the day. Even writing about this extreme drudgery exhausts me.

When Mum was four months pregnant, she and Mary arrived at Granny and Pop's together one Saturday afternoon and chatted happily about their pregnancies while preparing dinner. Their men were playing dominoes at the pub with Pop which left the women with plenty of time for a cuppa before dinner. As Mum crossed to the sink to fill the kettle, she suddenly slumped over with a sharp intake of breath and Mary rushed to her side.

Noticing Mum's face was chalk white, Mary helped her to a chair just as another gripping pain ripped through her belly. Knowing she was in trouble, Mum started to panic. Leaving Sandy with Mary and Granny, she staggered along the street to the local GP clinic. She knew him from her time living at Granny's.

As she entered the surgery, she was dismayed that there were no vacant seats and thought she might faint. A woman, seeing Mum's blanched face, stood to offer her seat, saying *"Hen, I'm next but you look awfie, so you go first."* As Mum was about to sit, the doctor poked his nose out of his room calling *"Next!"*

As she stood up after being examined, Mum was told that her body was threatening to miscarry the baby and she began to sob. While the doctor was still talking to her, she felt an intense pain and doubled over, only to see a rush of bright red blood gushing down her legs.

Grabbing a towel, the quick-thinking doctor unceremoniously rammed it up under her skirt, wedging it between her legs, and told the receptionist to call a taxi. He promised to come to the flat to see her after his surgery closed in an hour or so. Having no money in her purse for a taxi, she made her way slowly back to the flat with the towel still wedged between her legs. They were all white faced with worry when she arrived, and Alex carried her into the bedroom to get some rest.

When the doctor came, he gave Mum a more thorough examination in the bedroom and diagnosed pleurisy. He believed she was too unwell to carry a baby to term, saying that her baby's chances were very, very slim. He told her to go home to rest and have her regular doctor take it from there. Granny got her purse out of her handbag and gave them enough for a taxi home.

When her regular doctor arrived, he agreed that she was likely to miscarry any day now. At her desperate pleading, he conceded that with the right medicine, nourishing food and remaining bedridden for at least the next few months, there was a very slight chance everything could settle down.

How on earth Mum could rest with Sandy crawling around the flat all day, they wondered? If Alex didn't go to work, they wouldn't even be able to pay the rent. Nevertheless, they were determined to give this baby every chance of survival and put their heads together to devise a plan. Their plan was that Alex would make toast and tea in the mornings and then place Sandy, with his nappies and toys, on the bed beside Mum and head off to work, leaving sandwiches for their lunch.

Sandy toddled around the flat all day playing with his toys and Mum somehow managed to play with him on the bed. She was too scared to do more than get up to change his nappy or use the chamber pot. Arriving home around five, Alex pottered around making tinned soup with toast or baked beans on toast or even fried eggs for dinner. Unfortunately, he was hopeless at cooking, having always lived with his family, except in wartime, when the naval cooks fed him.

It's fair to say that he did try, but he liked to read his newspaper in the evenings, and only made half-hearted attempts at cleaning when absolutely necessary. He seemed totally unaware of the flat becoming increasingly messy and Mum's anxiety rose higher and higher as she daren't get out of bed to clean it.

Granny came once a week, taking two buses to get there, and would tidy up a little, but she wasn't a well woman herself so couldn't do more. Margaret, who had two young children by this time, also came by once a week, bringing a shepherd's pie or a small pot of soup with her on the bus and she would wash out the nappies leaving them on the pulley to dry.

***

A month passed, and despite everyone's best efforts, Mum became weaker, and began spitting up blood when she coughed. The doctor became increasingly worried, and the family advised her to get up out of bed and 'let the baby come away.' They tried everything to convince her, but she flatly refused; there was already one baby missing from her arms, and she wasn't going to allow another to be lost. She was almost five months pregnant; the baby was still there.

As she became ever more distressed at the prospect of staying in bed with no improvement to her health, the doctor came up with an idea. He said he would speak with her stepmother, Bessie, asking her to take Mum in for a time to strengthen her up. As one of the local Leith doctors, he knew her father and Bessie well and had often been invited to enjoy Sunday lunch with them.

Despite her own small flat being crowded, Margaret offered to take Sandy to her place for a few weeks to allow the doctor's plan to work. Mum was desperate enough now, she would do whatever it took to keep this baby, and she agreed. The kind doctor picked her up in his own car and drove her back to the house she had left on the eve of her wedding.

***

Bessie's wholesome cooking and the total bed rest didn't take long to work wonders! Within two weeks, she was feeling much better, despite missing her little family greatly. During those weeks, she had seen her father only once, when he had opened the door a crack, poked his head into the room and thrown an orange onto her bed.

Early in her third week there, the doctor advised her to begin taking short spells out of bed, firstly sitting and then walking slowly around the house to build her strength up. She followed his instructions to the letter and began walking around the room during the day or sitting by the kitchen fire and embroidering baby clothes. She was determined to be well enough to go home by her fourth week and decided it was time to begin helping around the house.

She was humming cheerily to herself when, after drying the dishes she was stacking them back into the built-in kitchen cupboard. As she placed the last plate on the shelf, she unexpectedly felt herself being grabbed from behind. Instinctively, she knew it was her father and felt the familiar cold fear rush through her body; she froze for a second, unable to think. He squeezed his body up against her back, blocking her inside the cupboard and grabbed her tightly around her swollen belly.

Her fury took over, and she fought back by squirming strongly and twisting herself around to face him. Looking at his face in disgust, she raised her arms to ward him off and yelled out for help. Bessie appeared at the door within a few seconds, but instead of stopping him, said dismissively *"Och, it's alright, that's just your faither."*

Mum pushed her arms hard against his chest and he stepped back in surprise. With room to get out, she squeezed past his body and rushed into the bedroom, slamming the door closed and leaning against it, gasping with a mixture of terror and rage. She wasn't his helpless victim any longer; she was a strong woman, a wife and mother now.

When her heart slowed and returned to normal, she made up her mind to leave the house as soon as she could, with or without the doctor's permission. When he arrived that afternoon, she pleaded with him to allow her to go home saying she was better and was missing her family so much. Her eyes filled with tears as she begged him, and he reluctantly agreed she could leave the next morning. His only proviso was that she had to take a taxi and have someone with her. Before leaving, he warned her this baby must be her last. She never told Alex what her father had done, as she was worried about his reaction. Although generally a peaceful man, he was likely to have given him a good thumping.

That night when Alex came to visit, Mum told him she was allowed to come home in the morning. As the next day was a Saturday, he would be able to help her to make the trip safely. Again, they couldn't afford a taxi and had to travel home by bus, with Alex clutching Mum's arm carefully the entire time. With butterflies in her stomach, she entered the flat, expecting to see the new paint he had promised to complete in time for her homecoming. However, the smile dropped from her face at the reality which greeted her. The small flat was a bit of a mess, with an unmade bed, grey sheets and the little cooker very grimy.

Paint brushes, paint pots and drop sheets were scattered everywhere, but at least the dishes had been washed and stacked to dry. Deflated and exhausted, she flopped onto the fireside chair and struggled to blink back her tears while he fussed around making a cup of tea and smiling from ear to ear. He was so happy to have her home she couldn't be angry and recovered quickly from her disappointment.

She gave herself a mental shake and pulled herself together, remembering she had arrived home a little earlier than planned and they impatiently waited for Margaret to arrive with Sandy. What mattered now was their baby had been saved and she was well again, their wee family was reunited and eagerly awaiting the arrival of their new addition.

***

Within a week of Mum's return, Sandy had a dreadful accident. He tipped boiling tea on his face and head from a teapot which had been placed on the gas ring to keep warm. He was walking now and had grown quite a bit taller over the last month, no one realised he could reach higher. In a panic,

Alex picked the hysterical boy up and ran his face and head under the cold tap while Mum screamed at him to stop.

She thought he should be plastering Sandy's face with butter, not water. They rushed to hospital, where the doctor commended Alex for his quick thinking and dressed the burns. Over the following month Mum made the long trek to the Sick Children's hospital with Sandy every day for treatment. There was a significant worry about possible damage to his eyes but thankfully he recovered well. With the worry and the daily travelling, she quickly lost the little fat she had gained while resting but did her best to stay well over the cold months ahead.

When her due date passed, along with the month of March, Mum began wondering if her labour would ever start. The unseasonably warm April sun arrived, and her labour started early on the afternoon of the third. Thankfully, Alex was home for lunch, and was about to leave for work when the first, strong pains grabbed her. Alex's sister Jeanie had offered to look after Sandy when Mum's time came so all three rushed there by bus. Jeanie's little daughter was playing happily on the floor with Sandy when Mum said a hurried, but teary goodbye.

In the bus heading for hospital, it became obvious to Mum that this baby was in a hurry, and she worried she may not make it in time, they would have to walk across a large grassy meadow before reaching the hospital and safety. As they struggled from the bus, she was moaning with pain and sweat stood out on her face despite the cold spring breeze.

Panicking, Alex didn't know what to do, so he flustered around her before deciding it would be best to take her mind off the pain. *"Oh hen,"* he said, *"let's sing a wee song while we walk."* Mum simply glared poisonous daggers at him, unable to talk, as pain and fear gripped her. She staggered on. When they reached the reception desk, he signed the proffered papers, kissed her hastily and turned to leave; men weren't allowed in labour rooms in those times.

When he reached the door, he turned back to see her seated in a wheelchair, her face white with pain, and he called out *"It's quarter past four hen, the wee one will be here at quarter past five."* The nurse shot him a scathing look, before whisking Mum away.

As labour was so advanced, Mum was taken straight to the delivery room where a wee straggly girl, weighing only five pounds, arrived safe and sound... at exactly five fifteen! You wouldn't believe it to look at me now but that tiny, scrawny baby she had fought so fiercely to keep, was me! I do believe Bessie's part in feeding Mum up with nutritious meals, and providing space for her to rest, had much to do with her return to health. And of course, with saving me! Despite her many faults, I'm thankful to Bessie because I'm here today to tell Mum's story.

Now a father of two, Dad was as proud as punch! He had a pigeon pair, a son and a daughter, and life was as grand as it could be! When he saw me for the first time later that night, he couldn't believe how much I looked like Mum, but actually my resemblance to him is more pronounced. We share the same sage green eyes, which change according to our mood. I have been so blessed to have been given Alex as my father; he was such a kind dad, who loved his children deeply, and never raised a hand to his children.

Dad in his naval uniform 1945

Mum and Dad. Wedding photo 24 December 1948

Mum and Dad enjoying Kinghorn Beach, our favourite family holiday destination

Pop and Granny Morrison at Kinghorn Beach 1950s

Mum, Sandy and I on holiday 1952

Mum's sisters, Agnes and Margaret with Sandy and I, 1952

*Mum and our dog Roy enjoying a little sun
in our back yard, Gilmerton 1960s*

Gilmerton, skipping in the street with my friends, I am the one skipping

Mum and Aunty Margaret at our farewell party

CHAPTER EIGHTEEN

1953 – 1956

With two growing children packed into the two small rooms, the flat was crowded and it became obvious that they needed to look for a better place to live. Sandy was an adventurous toddler and chafed at being cooped up in the flat most of the time and Mum struggled to get the large pram up and down the stairs to go shopping or to visit the play park for fresh air. Leaving the pram at the bottom of the stairs was impossible as it doubled as my cot when I grew too chubby for the little wash basket and, besides, it was a shared stairwell with the street door normally left open.

Leith, in those days, was a dodgy part of the city and the pram would probably be stolen if it was left there. It didn't take long until, once again, Mum was exhausted all the time, but she plodded on, so happy with her little family that even the recurrent bouts of bronchitis couldn't stop her.

One day, in 1954, Don's wife Betty told Mum about a woman she had met who was looking for a caretaker for the ladies boarding house she owned. The job included free rent on a roomy two-bedroom basement flat, a wage of two pounds ten shillings a month and free coal and electricity. In return, she required someone to clean the stairs of the four-story house, take buckets of coal up to each suite daily, hang out and bring in the laundry, and polish the brasses and stair banisters.

This sounded too good to be true but Mum nervously presented herself to the owner anyway. The woman was so impressed by her she offered Mum the job on the spot, saying she had interviewed some people who apparently thought cleaning was below them. This certainly was a win-win situation for them both. Mum and Dad hastily packed up our meagre furniture and belongings, and we moved into our new home in Bruntsfield, one of the classier parts of Edinburgh.

It was spring when we arrived, and we were super excited to see a large lawn and garden behind the house, accessed directly from the flat, so we could play outside when the weather was good. Sandy and I share fond memories of our Mum tying rags to our feet so we could skate along the hallway, giggling our heads off, and polishing the floor after she had washed and waxed it. I remember seeing her skating along in her thick woollen socks, demonstrating, her laughter echoing from the high ceiling. The smell of beeswax still takes me back to that lovely place and time.

To be able to run outside and tumble on the lawn or explore the garden was heavenly and Mum sometimes sat in the sun, enjoying a cup of tea while we played. The ladies upstairs were very kind and adored having us around, although we were given strict instructions not to bother them. I vaguely remember them peeking in the door to see if we were around, before they ventured out to play bridge or have lunch, and they sometimes brought us a wee bag of sweeties to share, a rare treat!

As spring rolled into summer, we all became stronger, healthier and happier. Mum was constantly busy, either keeping our flat clean or working in the main house, so Sandy and I were free to enjoy the garden or the spacious hallway when it was too wet outside. Summers in Scotland tend to be short-lived affairs, and autumn soon swept into the city, bringing cold, damp winds and rain with it. The old house was icy cold, and the basement damp.

Mum's cough returned and worsened along with the darkening skies. She struggled to keep up with the housework, especially carrying the heavy coal buckets up the four flights of stairs to the ladies' rooms. Sandy and I were frequently ill too, and the sound of coughing became the constant soundtrack to our lives. Our Dad was working on a job in the country, catching an early train on Monday mornings and returning late on Friday nights so he couldn't be around to help all week. Still, without rent to pay and an extra small wage coming in, their little savings account was growing.

Christmas arrived, bringing snow and icy conditions and, despite the coal fire which Mum kept roaring in the living room, the rest of the flat was bitterly cold and damp. It was a long and arduous winter that year, the coldest of the century, and we all experienced repeated bouts of illness, one after the other.

Summer arrived, bringing better health for us all, but Mum and Dad remembered the harshness of last winter and the toll it had taken on our health. They doubled their efforts to search for a new home. One warm July evening, Dad arrived home by train from his job in the country and Mum took his hand and gently told him Granny had been rushed to hospital. The family had been worried about her for some time as she was losing weight rapidly and had little or no appetite.

Jeanie had written to her sisters, Mary and Ina, who had emigrated to Canada following the Great Depression, to tell them about granny's illness. Ina rushed home to help, and everyone hoped for a full recovery. Sadly, despite resting every day, her condition worsened, and she was rushed to hospital after collapsing one afternoon.

Dad dashed to the hospital as soon as he heard and found Jeanie sitting beside Granny's bed. The doctors had said that their mother had suffered a tear in one of the tubes of her heart and was only expected to live for two or three days at the most. Over the next few days, the rest of the family took it in turns to sit with her, until she passed away a week later.

When his mother died, Dad was bereft, crying great heart-wrenching sobs alone in the bedroom. Mum said it was as though nothing would ever comfort him again after her death. She had been a good and faithful wife, mother, and grandmother, the heart and soul of her family, and with an empty nest, she and Pop had only just begun to experience life as a couple. Mum was also devastated, feeling that Granny was too young to die at only 68. She had taken Mum under her wing like a mother hen and had gently guided her in her new life as a wife and mother.

Ina cleaned the flat thoroughly before she left to return to her own family in Canada and while she was cleaning out the kitchen cupboards and drawers, found a box of pills with Granny's name on them. She wondered what they were for, as the tablets Granny needed for her blood pressure were kept on the bedside table. According to the local pharmacist, they were the weight loss pills which had been prescribed by her local doctor. Doctors at the time were calling them 'miracle' drugs as they really helped people to lose weight and Granny's high blood pressure was a worry with her stacking on the weight lately.

It took about a decade for those pills to be removed from the market as adverse side effects were being reported due to their main ingredient being an 'amphetamine,' or in other words, speed! A strong link had been found between the drug and heart attacks and the family were furious.

When Ina returned to her family in Canada, Pop was on his own in the now silent home which had always been filled with happiness. Never having been a man who cooked, he didn't even know how to boil an egg, happy to sit and read his newspaper while Granny bustled around looking after him and anyone else who popped in.

He was lost and lonely, what would happen to him now? The women in the family took turns to visit him during the day when they were able, bringing a meal and hoping to get him chatting, but it was mostly in vain. They would usually find him sitting by the fireside, staring into space, or sometimes beginning a sentence and looking over at Granny's empty chair for a response. His sons often popped in after work to take him to the local for a pint, and the family continued to gather there on a Saturday night, but the flat was so empty without dear Granny bustling around.

I have a little memory of my granny. She was a safe person to me, and I have a definite image of looking up at the rounded belly under her pinny, knowing she would pick me up. Her house was filled with food smells, warmth, and laughter. I wish I had been old enough to remember her more, but I was only three years old when she died.

***

In the months following Granny's death, autumn rushed in, and the nights gradually became dark and cold. Mum's health went downhill fast, and she developed pleurisy once again. With Margaret's help she struggled to keep up with her job during the week and Dad took over on weekends to give her a rest.

Before long, Sandy and I also developed bronchitis and the doctor advised us to move away from the cold, damp basement before the winter truly set in, warning that our lungs could be permanently weakened if we suffered through another winter there.

This was a terrible time for Mum, with bouts of illness dogging her and she worried she may not live to see us grow up. She often lay awake at night, terrified she would die while we were young and Dad would marry again, leaving us to be brought up by a stepmother – who of course would be wicked. Her sleeplessness added to her ill health, but she couldn't seem to relax.

Finally, she remembered the lessons she had learned in Sunday school about the all-knowing, loving God and she would beg Him every night, *"God, please let me live until my children grow up."* She felt as if her prayers were disappearing into thin air but hoped for the best; at least praying helped her fall asleep. One night, while she was praying, an idea popped into her head – *"Why don't we see if we can go and live with Pop again, I can look after him and we can have a warmer, drier place to live?"* Even with the coal yard and brewery to contend with, the small flat was at least warm and dry, unlike the basement flat.

Dad was thrilled with the idea, as he worried about his dad so much while he was away. When they asked if they could move back in, Pop was thrilled. We moved in as soon as we could, Mum and Dad back in their old bedroom and Sandy and I in the bed which took up the entire box room.

Pop was much happier with a full house again and within weeks, Dad was coming home every night because the job he was working on was now based in Edinburgh. After tea he would sit with Pop and play a game or two of chess, which sometimes drove Mum mad, but we were all comfortable and warm again. I loved living there, although the flat was a bit crowded. Sandy and I could play in the street when the weather wasn't too bad or even in one of the stairwells if it was raining or snowing.

I remember Mum telling me about the time I had fallen asleep in the stairway of another tenement building. She had been running around in a panic searching for me as I hadn't come home when she hung her head out of the kitchen window to call Sandy and I in. She asked a couple of the older girls from the street if they had seen me, and they told her I had been the baby in their game. Apparently, I had fallen asleep on the cold concrete, and they had left me there, covered in a coat. There were plenty of children to play with in the tenement area and we felt quite safe playing in groups.

On Thursday nights, Sandy and I joined most of the children in our street and walked up to the local church hall to attend the 'Band of Hope.' We looked forward to it every week. While there, we played games, sang some hymns and were given sandwiches and orange juice, with the occasional sugar bun thrown in. The people who ran the club were kind to us and it was great fun. At Christmas time there was always a party at which we were given presents, I still have a small doll I received, although she's one-armed now. Seemingly, it was run by the Women's Christian Temperance Union. The Union decried the use of alcohol and its effect on society, especially on women and children. A worthy objective, however, it's a good thing that they never came up to the flat on Saturday nights. Although there was only a little beer on offer, I think they would not have been impressed.

***

When Sandy turned five, he started at the local school and was excited about the upcoming adventure. On the first day of school, they set off, Sandy marching along in his uniform, and Mum nervously clutching his hand, trying to smile and be happy too. Her precious little boy was going to be out in the world, away from her protection. The closer they came to the gates, the more Sandy held back, slowing his walk, and when they reached the school door, he refused to go inside. Eventually, the head teacher came and impatiently plucked him up and with Sandy screaming, they disappeared along the hallway.

Horrified, she made her way home, blinded by tears, and walked back to see how he was at playtime. She hid herself from the children's view in a spot where she could see through the railings and eventually, over the sea of uniforms, spotted him standing by himself. He was leaning against a wall, rubbing his foot up against the opposite leg nervously; his head hanging down.

The other boys, who seemed to be very rough, were running around, shouting and kicking a ball, and they were deliberately bumping into him as they ran past. Her heart ached to see him looking so sad and afraid. Sandy was usually a happy boy, bright and adventurous, but also very sensitive. Both she and Dad believed he would settle down at school in time.

It wasn't to be. After Sandy arrived home in tears for the umpteenth time, telling Mum his teacher, a middle-aged woman, had shaken him until his teeth rattled. Mum decided she would visit the school the next day. She didn't take Sandy with her, leaving him with Pop and me, and headed to the school early.

When she arrived at the classroom and tried to speak with the teacher, she found herself on the receiving end of a loud and vicious tirade. The woman harangued her with stories of Sandy refusing to read aloud in the class, not answering her questions and usually not speaking to her at all. Mum stomped down the corridor to the head teacher's office and told her what had been going on, saying she would write to the local school superintendent if nothing was done. Asking around, she soon discovered many other parents had also complained.

Within a month, the local authorities investigated the teacher, they discovered she was unregistered and unqualified and was sacked. Good news, but this outcome did not help Sandy who by this time was suffering from severe anxiety. The family doctor sent him to see a child psychologist who, after doing a battery of tests, pronounced that he had a high IQ. He recommended another school for him and organised further testing there.

The school specialised in educating highly intelligent children and was situated in the beautiful old buildings of Moray House School, on the High Street of the city. Sandy quickly found his feet in this environment and flourished, much to everyone's relief. This was one of the many instances where Mum stood up for her children; she loved us more than life itself.

Mum returned to her old job part-time when I turned four, arranging with Pop to look after me, and preparing our lunch before she left in the morning. I use the term 'look after' but in truth Pop let me go about my own business, and I kept myself pretty amused. The job was only three days a week from ten to two pm. Financially, things improved with the added income but over the two winters we spent with Pop, illness continued to plague both Mum and Sandy. The doctor sent many letters to the Council, who oversaw the government rental properties, in an effort to get us into a proper house as soon as possible.

CHAPTER NINETEEN

1957

The long-awaited letter offering us a rental home finally dropped through the letterbox in the early spring of 1957. Mum danced around the kitchen when she opened it after work and Dad waltzed her around the room when he arrived home. Finally, the family could settle in their own little castle. With a choice of two houses, in the new suburb of Gilmerton, they made their choice. It was a two-story home, set in a block of four houses, with many identical blocks set on each side of the street, all the way down the crescent.

A 'two up - two down,' it had two bedrooms, a bathroom, a living room and a tiny kitchen. We were thrilled to see a small front garden, with a shiny entry door, a pathway leading around the house to a side door, and right through to the back garden. The savings account was just large enough to buy a brand-new, three-piece lounge suite, a dining setting, three beds and a rug. We couldn't wait to move in.

Leaving Pop alone again was difficult, but over the past two years living there, Mum and Dad had joined him into the local library; he was an avid reader. He had also joined a local pensioner group who held weekly activities and Pop had enjoyed a few outings with them. Of course, we would all continue to see him on Saturday nights, the highlight of the week, not only for him but also for the siblings and cousins in the family.

These nights followed much about the same pattern every time; the men would do their 'football pools' before heading off for a pint, while the Mums took turns at the cooker making tea for their families. The smell of frying was thick in the air, along with the women's chatter interspersed with occasional shrieks of laughter. After each family had taken a turn to sit at the table to eat, all the adults would squeeze around the table to play cards. I remember my eyes stinging and watering from the thick cigarette smoke as the night wore on.

There was a lot of laughter and noisy chatter, which we cousins added to by playing games, sometimes in the street or stairwell and other times in the bedroom. The was also much running in and out of the living room and it was total chaos. Sometimes there would be a baby asleep in the bottom drawer of Granny's old dresser, but when the other young kids drooped, we would all crowd into the double bed. We would lay 'head to toe,' often cowering under a pile of coats in terror, as the older kids terrorised us with ghost stories.

Eventually we would be rescued by the adults grabbing their coats and kids and rushing for the last bus home. Unfortunately, there were a few times when our little family would end up walking home after missing the last bus, as Dad would be reluctant to leave Pop. It was such a long walk, taking over an hour, but I'll never forget the feeling of gratitude to be breathing the fresh air into my lungs. I would take huge gulps, attempting to fill my lungs as fast as possible. That is when I made my decision never to become a smoker. During those seemingly endless walks home, Mum would be giving Dad the cold shoulder as he was always the last one out the door. Good memories!

***

We were thrilled with our new house, and at once set about making it into our own. We couldn't believe we had so much space, and Sandy and I loved our new twin beds. Our bedroom window looked out onto the back garden where Dad planted a vegetable plot. Mum planted flowers and shrubs in the front garden, and we quickly settled in our own space at last. The house seemed so big at the time, and it was, in comparison to the places we had previously lived, but when I visited Scotland as an adult and trailed through my old haunts, I had a little chuckle to see how small it is.

Gilmerton was quite a new suburb. It had initially been developed to house post-war families in the 'prefabs,' which were excellent little prefabricated houses. Designed to be only temporary, they were expected to last twenty years. These prefabs were being demolished during the latter part of the fifties and into the sixties to be replaced with permanent homes, like ours.

Many of the usable building materials were 'borrowed' during the night and ended up in the backyards of the new homes, including ours. Dad collected large slabs of concrete, embedded with pebbles, in his wheelbarrow over a series of nights and they became our new path.

With so many young families in the area, Sandy and I were quick to make friends and soon settled in. My best friend, Elsie Broom, lived next door to us and we were very close, her outgoing nature a perfect match for my shyness. Through our friendship, our mums became close too and were a wonderful support for each other throughout the ups and downs of life over many years. Mrs Broom, named Elsie like her daughter, was a beautiful soul, calm and efficient, and perfect for Mum.

The early days in our new home brought Mum's sense of humour to the fore and her relaxed mood led to Sandy and I playing some pranks on her, instigated by my big brother of course. One day, after we were sternly ordered to clean our room, we put some flour in a paper bag and balanced it on the top of the door which opened onto our built-in cupboard. We told her we had finished and asked her to come upstairs to inspect our hard work. She opened the door as expected, the flour packet fell and broke, narrowly missing her head, but puffing some flour onto her shoes.

She looked sternly at us and declared that we were to come downstairs for a good spanking. We placed books in our knickers before we went downstairs and, when we leaned over the arm of the sofa to receive our punishment, she proceeded to spank us on our square bums. How she held the laughter in, I don't know, but we all pretended that a genuine punishment had been given and we headed back to clean up the flour. This is the only prank I can clearly remember but there were a lot more at the time. Mum really was a great sport!

One thing that didn't change, even in this happy period, was hearing Mum and Dad argue. When Dad was at home, it was as though he wasn't there in a way, keeping to his quiet little routines, reading the newspaper or, when we eventually got a TV, watching football. Mum used to goad him into an argument and when we felt it coming, we would scatter as fast as we could.

Sometimes, I would hear them shouting at night when I was in bed, and I would climb over into Sandy's bed for a cuddle. I was afraid Mum would leave us for good. We would often hear her shout *"I'm leaving"* or *"No man will ever keep me down again"* as she flew out of the house, slamming the door behind her, only to slip home a while later. She had nowhere to go really.

I can clearly recall one argument in particular; it was during an afternoon in the summer. Mum was shouting loudly about something, and Dad was hissing at her to be quiet, so she went around the house opening every window. As she opened each window, she stuck her head out and screamed "Fire!" loudly.

On the radio recently there had been a story about a person screaming "Help!" while being attacked in their own home and no one had come to their aid. So, she had decided that screaming 'fire' would be better. That incident seems hilarious now, but it was not at all funny to us at the time, so embarrassing!

Mum continued to faint at the most inconvenient times, such as when Sandy and I returned home after school, reviving her was such an inconvenience! On the rare occasion she and Dad went to a fancy party, she would drink only one or two glasses of sherry and lemonade all night. It was all they could afford, even if she had wanted to drink more. She and Dad would glide around the room, waltzing gracefully in each other's arms, they certainly complemented one another.

Sadly, though, there were many times when the heat in the room and her excitement would cause her to collapse. As she came to her senses again, she would be dreadfully embarrassed, realising that the partygoers who didn't know her would assume she was drunk.

Gilmerton was a great place to grow up. Every summer, all the girls in our little neighbourhood group would hold a 'back green' concert in aid of charity. We would plan and rehearse for weeks, sometimes including a boy or two if necessary. We scheduled singing acts, dancing acts and the occasional poetry recitation, Robert Burns was always a favourite. Some of the Mums would help us make simple costumes and others would bake some fairy cakes to sell on the day. After a couple of arguments, our decision-making improved, and we would soon be ready for the big day. A few sheets would be set up on the clothes lines as curtains in our chosen garden and the concert would begin.

We usually made a decent amount, and one year raised almost two pounds. As it was a large sum, we decided to take it ourselves to the Princess Margaret Rose hospital, chosen because it specialised in helping crippled children. The Matron was very thankful and invited us to stay for afternoon tea in her office. We enjoyed more cake and orange juice than our two pounds could possibly have bought and left there feeling very proud of ourselves.

CHAPTER TWENTY
1958 – 1964

After living in our lovely new home for a year, Mum began thinking about how perfect it would be if another baby was added to our family. She missed the patter of tiny feet, especially with all the mod cons we now enjoyed, so there appeared to be no reason why not. However, Dad quickly reminded her of a pertinent reason: the warning she was given not to have any more children after her difficult pregnancy with me.

Mum refused to accept that her health should stop them, and she set about working all her persuasive charms on poor Dad. He didn't stand a chance! Soon enough, they were thrilled to discover that Mum was pregnant again, *"It will be so different this time,"* she promised Dad when she broke the news: we have fresh air, hot water and plenty of room. Dad was happy with his life, with a wee house, a wee wife and soon a wee family of three children, just perfect!

This pregnancy, once again, proved to be a difficult one. Bronchitis and pleurisy plagued Mum and as her health declined, so did her weight. She was continually exhausted and suffered from more fainting turns than usual, leading to everyone worrying she would harm the baby in a fall. I remember one fall that happened when she was around six months pregnant.

She'd been arranging flowers at the living room window and stepped back to see their effect, little realising that our dog was lying behind her. She fell back heavily and landed with a terrible thud. When Sandy and I revived her, she spent the rest of the afternoon in bed, afraid for her baby.

At thirty-four weeks, she was admitted to hospital for complete bed rest and was told she would have to stay there until after the birth. Arrangements were hurriedly made for Sandy and me to live with Dad's sister Jeanie, who lived close by.

Over the time she was hospitalised, Dad popped into Jeanie's house for dinner at night before heading to visit Mum and returning to our own home to sleep. It was such a long time to spend without our Mum and, although we played happily with our cousins and were well cared for, we missed our parents so much. Sandy and I were 8 and 6 respectively. Children were banned from visiting maternity hospitals in those days. I would often hide away somewhere and write Mum little notes with tears in my eyes.

Seeing how distressed her sister was becoming by not being able to see her precious children, Auntie Margaret picked us up one day and took us to the hospital. During her last visit, she had arranged for Mum to come out onto the balcony to see us, and we stood for a while looking up to the second floor until she came out and waved, like the Queen. In the end, it was obvious this had been a bad idea, as we all became distressed. I remember sobbing as I looked up at her, so far away from us. Mum was so distressed that she was given a pill to calm her down after we left.

The weeks without our Mum dragged along with agonising slowness until eventually Dad appeared unexpectedly at Auntie Jeanie's house to tell us that we had a new baby sister, Catherine! We thought the news meant Mum and our new sister would be home the next morning but were disappointed to hear we would have to be patient for two more weeks.

The wait felt like years. The big day arrived, and I clearly remember everything; blue skies greeted us as Sandy and I packed our clothes into our school bags and ran to the corner of the street where our auntie and uncle lived. Hopping from foot to foot, we peered impatiently along the main road for the actual taxi that Mum, Dad, and our new sister would be travelling home in. We screamed and waved like crazy when the shiny black car turned the corner and passed right by us. I saw Mum's face pressed up against the window as she waved frantically, her eyes wet with tears. As soon as it passed us leaving a cloud of exhaust behind, we turned and ran like the wind all the way home, school bags bumping on our backs.

As we turned the corner into our street, we saw the taxi pull away from the house. We ran down the hill to our gate and, panting, burst through the door and straight into Mum's arms. There were tears streaming down my face and my nose was snotty by the time I let go, and I reckon Sandy was the same.

Placing her hands on our shoulders, Mum stood us back a little to look into our eyes, exclaiming at how we had grown.

She pointed to the white basket sitting on top of the radiogram in the corner of the living room and placed her finger to her lips to shush us. We crept quietly over to peek in and met our new baby sister for the first time. Catherine was beautiful, so perfect, with the softest skin I had ever touched.

I loved her blue eyes and chubby cheeks immediately. When she grasped my finger tightly in her hand as though she would never let go and looked up at me, I was smitten. Home felt perfect for the next week or so as visitors buzzed in and out, bringing silver coins to place into Catherine's hand for luck and cute little knitted booties and matinee jackets.

They would peek in to see my sister, declare that she was gorgeous, cluck over her, enjoy tea, biscuits, and cake, and leave again. It was simply wonderful, I felt proud to be a big sister, no longer the baby of the family and felt quite the celebrity myself. We were not to know then, that when all the visitors departed, the vacuum they left behind would be filled by dark, gloomy shadows in Mum's mind.

***

When all the visitors and congratulations ended, an unaccountable despondency gradually came over Mum. Arriving home from school, I would see she was somehow not right; now I understand she had probably been crying during the day. She kept up a brave front most of the time and loved and cared for Catherine, but she was short tempered and likely to snap irritably at Sandy and me. Writing about this time later, she said, "*I didn't know what was wrong, well everything was, especially me*".

She couldn't see her way back to happiness. Logically, she knew her life had never been so perfect: a cosy little home, a loving, gentle husband and now three beautiful children, she should be grateful. *"Just pull your socks up and get on with it"* was normally her mantra so she must have been devastated by her inability to pull herself up.

With the burden of this intense sadness, Mum's health plummeted yet again, and she resorted, guiltily, to sleeping at various times during the day. Despite her constant exhaustion, she always hauled herself into the kitchen to make dinner for her family and somehow managed to keep the household going, her mask firmly in place.

Kids know, on some level, when the atmosphere in the home isn't right, even though the daily routine seems undisturbed on the surface. I remember withdrawing into myself, trying to escape the heavy, insecure atmosphere by crawling behind the sofa to read quietly. Mum would be cross when she tracked me down; reading was not a pastime she understood as her father would never have put up with such idleness. I didn't have many books of my own and the ones I did have were gifts from my lovely Auntie Margaret. She bought me an Annual every Christmas. I loved the 'Bunty' which also brought out a weekly magazine which sometimes I would be able to buy with my pocket money.

Every birthday I would receive a book from Auntie too, and I can remember the feeling of pleasure I had when opening a new book. I would savour the smell, before delving eagerly inside, to lose myself in the story. When I went to play with my cousin Joan, I was always so jealous of her awesome collection of books; Rupert Bear was one of my favourites. As I grew older, books grew to become my greatest friends, and still are. Sandy coped by escaping to the outdoors to play with his mates as often as possible, only coming home when he had to. The streetlights were our cue to hurry home and we both remember the feeling of anxiety building, expecting to be in trouble for something when we arrived.

While writing about this period, I realise that this was the period when I was having a great deal of trouble at school. Although Moray House suited Sandy perfectly and he was thriving there, it wasn't a good place for me. I didn't cope well with their teaching methods. I felt like a failure, and often hid myself in a toilet cubicle for ages refusing to come out when I was missed. Eventually, some unfortunate teacher would have to climb past the sectional wall from the next cubicle by climbing across the window ledge to unlock my door.

I also stole money from other children's blazer or raincoat pockets, I don't know why as I knew it was wrong. Clearly, I was not coping at all well for a while there but happily my behaviour improved after about a year. In year five, I moved to a school in Gilmerton where both my happiness and my grades picked up rapidly.

Post-natal depression was not generally spoken about in those days. All the old wives knew of the 'baby blues' which came and went in the days after birth, but Mum's protracted depression went far beyond the baby blues. Thankfully, when Catherine was about nine months old, the cloud thinned and eventually lifted altogether. Mum genuinely smiled again, thank God, and everyone could breathe at last. We never spoke of the situation at the time, it was simply the way things were. It wasn't until I was a struggling new mother myself that Mum talked with me about 'the blues' and how badly she had suffered with depression for such a long time.

With Mum's spirits lifted, the family settled down into a happy routine, and life was good. Sandy and I had friends and outside activities, were settled into school and we even went on camping holidays in summer. Catherine was a delightful wee sister and when she was around two, I moved into the double bed in the front bedroom to share with her. Mum and Dad were consigned to the sofa bed in the living room as Sandy was now to share his bedroom with Pop who had become increasingly 'dithery' as he aged.

Dad's siblings eventually set up a roster whereby each family would take care of him for six, often trying, months. Those months could occasionally be difficult as he grew quite cantankerous as he aged. I remember him occasionally refusing to eat, saying that his meal was full of poison. He read all the newspapers faithfully and was aware of the so-called 'chemical revolution' that gripped agriculture following WW2. Time has shown him to be correct in his theories, with dangerous chemicals such as DDT being sprayed on our food 'willy nilly'.

***

Dad and Jeanie's husband, Harry, were constantly devising ways to make money. One scheme sounded so perfect that they decided to go into business. They bought a small, enclosed wagon and fitted it out with shelves. Once it was filled with supplies, they were ready to begin their mobile grocery store. The horse was stabled at a farm close by, and Dad, who was great with animals, became solely responsible for the horse's daily welfare.

The mobile store travelled through the streets of Gilmerton, Hyvots, Liberton and other close suburbs which were only serviced by the occasional small corner shop. The business demanded long days, six days a week for Dad. He fed the horse at dawn, hitched up the wagon, loaded the cart, and was on the road by nine o'clock, and would reverse the process at the end of the day.

Sadly, it soon became obvious that the business wasn't making the profit they had dreamed of and was bringing in only enough for supplies, essentials for the horse and Dad's small wage. One of the problems was Dad's kind heart, which would see him pop an extra few potatoes or pound of flour into a harassed housewife's shopping basket. This was especially true if she arrived with a large brood of bairns hanging around her skirts. He couldn't stand to see the snotty-nosed children stare up at him wistfully without handing them a wee sweetie.

A kind heart is a wonderful thing; however, it doesn't bode well for business profits. It all ended badly when Dad became ill, diagnosed with complete mental and physical exhaustion, and was practically bedridden for weeks. He couldn't even get himself out of bed to go to Social Security and apply for the dole, much to Mum's absolute fury and dismay.

The relationship between the two business couples remained strained for about a year but eventually they put it all behind them and became friends for the remainder of their lives. The failed business became the precursor to some massive changes in the lives of both families.

***

The 'swinging sixties' had set in and there was much optimism for a bright, exciting future. The early years of the sixties however, also heralded some frightening times, with the terror of the Cuban crisis, followed by President John F Kennedy's assassination and the death of Marilyn Monroe.

Racial riots were taking place in the United States, and we watched in awe as Martin Luther King gave impassioned speeches on our black and white televisions before he too was assassinated. Young people began to feel their emerging ability to change the world, and we wore 'ban the bomb' badges and t shirts, some of us not really understanding what all this turmoil meant.

On a brighter side, Wednesday nights became the most anticipated night of the week to watch TV. Top of the Pops started in 1964 and we watched Gerry and the Pacemakers, Cliff Richard, the Rolling Stones, Dusty Springfield and other musical heroes with our mouths agape. 'Beatlemania' took hold of the world and led us into new territory, and we all had a favourite Beatle or Rolling Stone.

I was consumed with jealousy when a teenage neighbour landed a job with Radio Luxembourg where she would be able to meet some of these stars. Tuning in to the pirate stations on our 'trannies' was how we listened to pop music, and Elsie and I would walk to Girl Guides belting out all the latest hits. The world was opening up its doors to me as I turned twelve.

Even during these good years, Mum would succumb to severe bronchitis or pleurisy every winter and would faint at the drop of a hat. She was offered the chance to have her dicky mitral valve replaced with a pig's valve but decided against it, as the surgery was still experimental. It was just as well really, as many recipients of the pig valves died within a couple of years.

Mum's greatest fear was dying before her children were grown. In 1963, her dear sister and defender, Agnes, became gravely ill with cancer. Aunty Margaret and Mum visited her as often as possible. As Mum watched on helplessly, her fear of dying and leaving us behind worsened.

The treatments Aunty Agnes was being given didn't appear to be working and she was consumed with worry about her little boy, Ian. Fortunately, Uncle Don and Aunty Betty agreed to adopt him, and she held on, despite her terrible pain, until the legal paperwork was finalised. Sadly, she passed away in August 1963. The family were devastated at the loss of their brave sister.

***

I remember those years in Gilmerton Dykes as the happiest years of my childhood and am sure Catherine and Sandy feel the same. We were all very settled and Dad, not being particularly ambitious, was happy and contented with his life, coming home from work to his wee wife and wee family, kissing Mum and then reading his newspaper quietly. He played chess with Pop on Wednesday nights and enjoyed a few pints with his mate on a Saturday night after watching his beloved "Heart of Midlothian" football team play.

Little did we know then that we were all about to be flipped upside down, literally!

CHAPTER TWENTY ONE

1964 – 1967

After the mobile grocery business failed, Harry and Jeanie really struggled to settle, and the family left for a new life in Australia in 1963. This was during the period of the '£10 Pom', where it only cost ten pounds each to migrate to Australia or New Zealand. Australia was marketed strongly, highlighting the advantages for families: plenty of work, good housing and best of all, abundant sunshine. All very tempting during the cold Scottish winter.

Letters from Australia arrived, telling us how well they had settled in and how they were enjoying life in their new country. Our cousin Jean was enthusiastic about the sunshine, the fresh fruit, the space everywhere and the freedom she was enjoying. She included a plan of their new house, and we were astonished to see that it contained three bedrooms, living room and kitchen, and a 'laundry' room to boot. We had never heard of a whole room being set aside to do your washing!

After spending a few months in Pennington Migrant Hostel, situated in the west of Adelaide, South Australia, they moved twenty miles north to the fast-growing satellite city of Elizabeth. This blossoming town was established to house those who worked in the factories there and all the homes were initially built by the housing trust. The largest factory was General Motors Holden which employed thousands of local people. There were many other factories, some of which produced components for Holdens; the area was booming.

The letters Jeanie sent to her brothers were filled with praise for Elizabeth, and, although Dad was generally content with life, Mum was more ambitious. She could see the opportunities a new life in Australia may hold, especially for her children. After all, what's not to love about endless sunshine, good jobs, and good schools? Over the following year, the three brothers began to seriously consider emigrating and their wives soon came on board with the idea.

Everyone was swept up in the optimism of the moment and the men trotted off to Australia House together to apply, including Pop in the application. Sandy, Catherine, and I were incredibly excited by the prospect of a trip around the world. We had never travelled any further than Scarborough in the north of England. The adventure beckoned like something from the movies.

In her letters, our cousin Jean described her journey to Australia by ship in wonderful detail. She boasted of a swimming pool, many decks with games sections, lots of food, activities such as Bingo or cards, daily movies and even dances or balls for the adults. It all sounded incredible, and I could hardly wait for our sailing date. We had some new clothes for the journey - swimming suits, shorts and dresses - and Mum and Dad were rigged out too. Our sailing date was confirmed, only five months away.

There followed months of frantic activity, selling our furniture, packing and organising everything; we had to be ready when the big day arrived. Devastatingly, during this time Pop took a bad turn and fell, hitting his head on an electric fire. This was the first time I experienced deep loss and grief. The whole family were shattered, and when I heard the gut-wrenching sound of Dad sobbing, my heart broke for him. The sound of racking, painful cries coming from the bathroom echoed around the house chilling me to the bone. I felt as though it must be the end of the world.

I loved Pop, my quiet, gentle grandfather, and was devastated when the adults left for the funeral, leaving Sandy and I behind to look after Catherine. In those days it was believed that protecting children from the sadness of the day was the best idea, but I wonder if it was really so they could attend the wake. I struggled with the way he disappeared from my life with no goodbye as though he had simply ceased to be. We kids weren't told very much about Pop's death and felt as though our own sorrow didn't matter.

***

It was almost time to leave, and all the talk was of the big sailing day. Harry and Jeanie were working hard to organise houses for us to rent when we arrived in Australia. She said that Pennington Migrant hostel, where most migrants went on arriving in Adelaide, wasn't the best start for us. I've since spoken with other people of my age who migrated around the same time, and they loved the hostel life, so I reckon we actually missed out.

A large wooden crate was soon picked up from our house. It was packed with our most precious items, including our best woollen coats and winter shoes, some linens and special dishes and the few prized toys or books we were allowed to bring. When the sailing date was almost upon us, a letter arrived to say that there was trouble brewing in the Suez Canal and ships would not risk the trip.

Our options were to cancel the whole venture, travel by aeroplane or wait for a sailing date sometime in the future. At this late stage we couldn't possibly wait, as everything had been either packed or sold and our notice given on our council house, so flying it was to be, much to everyone's disappointment.

In her writing, Mum explains those final days in Scotland as terrifying. The whole family were going about their allocated cleaning tasks when she stumbled upon Dad, slumped down in the middle of the staircase, head in hands. Worried, she asked if he was OK, and he replied *"Are we doing the right thing hen? It's an awfie long way and we can't be coming back again for at least two years if we don't like it."*

So angry she was speechless for a second, Mum eventually blurted, *"It's a bit late now to be thinking that isn't it? We've no furniture, no job and no home!"* I remember hearing her shouting and felt so sorry for Dad, having been on the wrong end of her razor-sharp tongue many times myself. I carried on cleaning as though I hadn't heard the shouting. I remember a feeling of fear and sorrow overtaking my previous excitement. Saying goodbye to our little terrier, Roy, left me with a sore heart and my feelings intensified over our last days.

We stayed with family on our final days in Edinburgh and saying goodbye to the aunties, uncles and cousins I would be leaving behind, possibly forever, was devastating. I was already feeling sad over leaving my best friend Elsie behind. In truth, we didn't expect to see any of them ever again, Australia was so far away, and travel was too expensive to contemplate for the likes of us.

The big night arrived, and on the 26th of October 1965, Edinburgh Waverley station witnessed the influx of our family who gathered on platform 20, ready for the night train to London. We were dressed in our best clothes. Our family, Dad's brothers and their families formed quite a crowd, 16 in all.

The Morrison family's mass exodus even attracted the attention of the press who took photographs of us to go alongside a short article. After the long overnight train ride, sitting up in the carriage, we finally arrived at Kings Cross station at six am. Unsure how to get to the airport for our flight, the brothers left the station to investigate, and we ended up in a taxi bus on our way to London Heathrow.

With our first closeup view of the aeroplanes, we children were awestruck by their size, although compared to today's jumbos, they were tiny. The nervous anticipation overtook us all once again. We expected some level of luxury on the plane, but our hopes were dashed, as we squeezed into our cramped seats to begin the flight from hell. Smoking was allowed in those days, so my eyes were constantly stinging, the food was terrible and one of the engines on the wing next to Sandy and I caught fire and in terror we watched the flames rushing by us.

Despite reassurances from the crew that all was well, we made an emergency stop in Kuwait for repairs. The waiting area was a cockroach-infested, blisteringly hot tin shed with hard bench seats around the walls, the ceiling fans did nothing but move the hot air around our sweltering bodies. I remember being terrified of the men in their long tunics and puzzled over why they wore 'tea towels' on their heads. All the children kept close to their parents on our long stop there.

Walking into the airconditioned airport in Darwin, we were relieved to be greeted by our cousins, John, and Ken, who were working in Darwin at the time. We sat in the cool air, sipping cold drinks and listening with rapt attention as they regaled us with countless stories of their travels in this strange land. We felt that we had finally arrived. What we didn't realise was that there was still a six-hour flight ahead before our journey would end in Adelaide.

We finally stepped off the plane on the night of the 30th of October 1965, four long days after leaving Edinburgh. I remember the joy of seeing my auntie, uncle and cousins again. All sixteen of us were ushered into a convoy of cars and we travelled to the brand-new city of Elizabeth. Squashed together in the cars, we drove for miles into the dark countryside before finally reaching a flat plain with scattered bungalows.

I remember Mum's dismayed face as she realised how far from the city we would be living. Finally clambering out of our vehicle, we felt dirty, exhausted, and shell-shocked and stood outside a door waiting for Dad to unlock it. He was so tired that the keys jangled uselessly in his hands. This house was to be home to twelve of us for the time being, our family of five and Dad's brother, George and his family of seven.

There were three bedrooms and one bathroom and it was furnished with odds and sods of furniture, kindly donated by the local Scottish community. These people were a wonderful support to us in the early days, helping us to settle into our new lives 'down under.' In those days, Elizabeth housed many migrant families as well as Australians, all working together in the local businesses. It was generally a friendly and supportive place to live, although a few pockets had more trouble than others.

With four adults and eight children squeezed together in such a small house, life promised to have its challenges. I'm not sure what the adults felt at this time, but this new adventure was thrilling for us. That first night, as Mum and Auntie Mary put the youngest kids off to bed, we older ones lay on the dark lawn experiencing the absolute foreignness of our new surroundings, breathing in warm air that felt like velvet. The exotic night smells, the oppressive heat and the constant symphony of crickets surrounded us as we stared in awe at a sky so dark the stars blazed like diamonds. This place was a wonder to us.

Finally collapsing into bed in the room that would be home to all four girls, sleep evaded us as we were overtired and so hot. Opening the windows only helped a little as we were shocked to find on raising the glass pane, that a thick, slightly rusty wire grid followed it. Never having seen flywire before, we were annoyed at the way it blocked the slight breeze but soon understood. While lying outside on the lawn earlier we had vaguely noticed a high-pitched whining and some little pin pricks on our bodies but were unaware the mosquitoes were feasting on our blood. We spent the night scratching until we bled.

At dawn, we woke to a sky so bright we had to squint our eyes to see. It was such a dazzling blue, and everything appeared vivid in the sun's glare. We ran around the yard exploring every nook and cranny and eating fruit straight off the tree for breakfast, the juice dribbling down our chins. We had never tasted anything so delicious in our lives. Britain was not part of the European Common Market in those days and any fruit more exotic than apples, pears and berries were a rare treat. We headed off to explore the neighbourhood, running around the streets barefoot and marvelling at the houses we saw, they were so different to 'home.' Our first days in this strange foreign land were electrifying, promising so much. It didn't take long for the shine to wear off.

Dad and Uncle George went out each day looking for work, wearing their suits and hats as was protocol in Scotland; heads up, chest out, armed with good references. The daily trudge in the heat soon wore them down as they slogged from place to place, and they would pop in for a cold beer when a pub beckoned, basically ending the search for the day.

Auntie Mary and Mum were busy stocking the pantry, cooking, cleaning and crazily killing ants, mozzies, and flies. It was as if these bugs were determined to take over the house and we lived with the constant smell of fly spray in our noses.

The Mums walked around the house a couple of times a day with the hand-held Mortein pump spray, madly pumping lethal poison into the air. The floor was constantly slick with the oily residue from the heavy droplets of Mortein landing there. I suppose the bug wars were inevitable with eight kids running around the house.

One unforgettable memory is of baby Brian, screaming blue murder from outside the back door. Mum and Auntie were horrified to find him covered in ants from head to toe, literally black with them, as he had been put outside in his pushchair with a 'slippery sam' ice block to eat.

They unclipped him and rushed into the bathroom, where they shoved him under the cold running water in the bath until the ants were washed off. After all the drama, he was found to have the plastic tube from the ice block still clutched in his little fist; he wasn't going to miss out on his last little bit of sweetness.

For some reason, our parents decided to send us to school, perhaps not realising the school year was about to end. This caused extra stress for everyone, as the task of finding second-hand school uniforms and books meant the costs kept eating into our savings.

At school, in typical Aussie style, the kids around us shortened everyone's name, whether we liked it or not. I became Pam, pronounced in nasal tones, and Catherine became Cathy. It seemed as though along with our friends and belongings; we had left our sense of who we were in Scotland and felt the pressure to be someone different in this strange place.

The truth is, we would have been fine without school for the last weeks of the year, and I certainly would have been glad. Going to Elizabeth Girls Technical High was a shock to me, so different from my school at home, and I struggled to make friends. The hateful girls in my class laughed at my Scottish accent, saying they couldn't understand a word I said so I shed my Scottish brogue quickly to try to blend in, something I truly regret to this day.

With eight kids in the house, we were not short of playmates. We had been given a rusty old three-wheeler bike with a seat on the back for a passenger and many hours were spent playing 'buses' with the younger kids. Another game we girls played in our room was 'schools,' my cousin Lorraine and I were teachers, and we made the younger kids sit in rows, using our suitcases as desks. These cases also served as our wardrobes containing all our clothes and worldly goods.

We managed to get along most of the time but being constantly squashed together presented us all with many challenges. For instance, Cathy, who was 7 and could never bear to see any animal hurt, decided to poison our cousin John, who was 5. She noticed him using a magnifying glass to blow up ants and decided to put a stop to it. Her ingenuous mind came up with the idea of mixing washing powder with water to resemble slightly melted ice cream, a rare treat.

She offered the bowl to him with a spoon and waited impatiently for him to gobble it down. Thankfully he had the good sense not to eat it and no harm was done, I think he even stopped blowing up the ants for fear of his life. Head lice decided to make their presence felt in a big way and we were constantly having our hair treated with disgusting, oily stuff and combed through with a tiny comb which took out more hair than nits.

Money was tight, the men had picked up a little casual work, but the parents were fearfully watching as the pennies shrunk day by day. With all this pressure, it wasn't surprising when tensions overflowed, and, in the cramped home, our parents started to quarrel. Auntie Mary and Uncle George shared a bedroom with the baby and Mum and Dad's bed was in the L shaped lounge/dining room, so there was no real privacy for the couples.

The mums managed to get along quite well, as did the dads, but marital harmony in the house disintegrated. A couple of times I heard the frightening sound of muffled shouts and scuffles coming from Auntie and Uncle's room during the night, and often heard Mum trying to keep her voice low as she hissed at Dad to stop spending precious money on beer.

Christmas arrived quickly and we were warned that we wouldn't be getting Christmas presents, a tree or decorations this year, there was no money. The children went to bed on Christmas Eve, feet dragging. However, when we woke up, we found that a couple of gifts had magically appeared at the bottom of our beds, and there was a fully decorated Christmas tree in the lounge, complete with lights. It felt like a miracle to us.

The Scottish community from the Caledonian club provided everything; a gift for each child, the decorated tree and even Christmas dinner, I will never forget their kindness. There was also a gift from Auntie Jeanie and family, one from

Cousin Jean, and a small one from Mum and Dad too. We could hardly believe it!

***

The new school year commenced, and we were still all cramped into the stifling hot house together. Arriving home from school, we often found Mum lying on the bed, with a wet flannel draped across her forehead. Her heart condition meant she suffered greatly from the heat, and we all thought it was only the heat that was getting her down. She managed to hold it together most of the time, but looking back, I see that she was rapidly falling into depression and despair.

***

It seemed as if we would never be in a home of our own. We had expected to be cramped together for about three or four months, but the time dragged on and the tension between the adults grew unbearable. Dad and uncle were still working on the railways on a casual basis and often arrived home late for dinner, smelling of beer.

Mum blamed Uncle George for being a bad influence on Dad but I know it wouldn't have taken any persuading to get him into the pub, the beer was cold. They had worked hard all day in the scorching heat and must have been thirsty and dirty.

The tension finally exploded one disastrous night when the men came home from work, late again and smelling of beer. I was in the lounge room next to the kitchen at the time, and could hear Mum angrily chopping the vegetables, when Uncle George stepped into the kitchen. There was muffled conversation and suddenly the chopping stopped, and I heard a scuffle and bump, followed by raised voices.

Dad ran into the kitchen, and everything went quiet. Seconds later, he led a rather dazed-looking Mum to bed, and I made myself scarce. Years later Mum told me about that day; she said when Dad appeared in the kitchen, it was to find his brother backed into a corner with Mum standing before him. She held a sharp knife clenched in her hand, pointed right at his stomach. I was so shocked to hear this that I didn't ask her what had happened to make her act so violently.

At the time, as children, we could only sense that the atmosphere in the house, tense before the knife situation, was now positively leaden. Both couples were no longer on speaking terms. Mum had always been a volatile woman but now she and Dad were constantly at loggerheads. As children, we did our best to keep out of the way; a difficult task with twelve people squashed together in the little house.

Thankfully, within weeks, the house emptied out as Uncle's family were allocated a house in Elizabeth West and we could all breathe. The short time we were supposed to be squashed together had stretched to almost eight months.

With the house now our own, and the lounge room no longer Mum and Dad's bedroom, a rental TV set appeared, how exciting! Two easy chairs, a sofa and coffee table arrived in a trailer, bought from 'Hazel's' second hand store in Smithfield. Many immigrants in the 1960s setting up house in Elizabeth will remember trekking off there in search of cheap furniture, usually in a borrowed car with trailer attached. The hot and dusty trip along Main North Road to the store would take ages, and we traipsed around the dusty, hot shed to unearth what we needed.

Cheap and cheerful was the order of the day, in fact the cheaper the better. Mum was a whiz at bringing wooden furniture pieces back to life, and even the dustiest, scratched piece would be transformed in a matter of minutes with soap and water, vinegar, beeswax, and good old-fashioned elbow grease.

Finally, nine months after our arrival in oz, we were lucky to be offered a house and were relieved to move into the tiny housing trust home in Elizabeth Grove, directly opposite Cathy's school. It had three bedrooms, a lounge, kitchen/diner, bathroom and laundry. It was a relief to finally feel settled. Cathy and I were so pleased to set up the bedroom we would share, lovingly retrieving our books and toys from the crate which had arrived from Scotland a few weeks earlier.

Although a few precious things were broken, we were so happy to see our few treasured possessions again, placing our little ornaments and books onto our dressing table. As we now had a front and back garden, Dad used the crate to make a cubby house for Cathy who spent many happy hours playing in it with her friends.

CHAPTER TWENTY TWO

1968-1978

Our second summer in Australia rolled around and, as the heat built up in our house, Mum spent more and more time in bed. As we were renting our house, we couldn't install air-conditioning, besides most houses weren't air conditioned in those days. We all sweltered. Most mornings she couldn't drag herself out of bed even to see Cathy off to school. Doing her own hair, packing her recess, and leaving the house silently became the normal morning routine for her. Sandy and I having left earlier as our schools were further away.

When Cathy arrived home for lunch, Mum would be up and about with lunch ready. I feel so sad to think of my little sister heading off to school without even a kind word. We all left the house this way, never daring to wake Mum up, all hell would break loose if we did, but Cathy was only around eight at the time.

We didn't really think too much about the situation, just accepted it, as we were quite used to Mum's need for sleep and her recurring illnesses. We had all learned from a young age never to wake Mum up in the mornings. Her tongue lashings were something we dreaded. We would rather receive a good spanking than feel the bite of her tongue as her words hurt in a way that no slapping ever could.

What we didn't realise, of course, was that she was deeply depressed. We knew nothing about depression in those days and, besides, we were all busy with our own issues as we struggled to fit into our new lives. Cathy has always been able to light up a room with her presence and she quickly made lots of school friends. It wasn't long before she also began studying ballet, she was a very graceful dancer just like Mum and she was surrounded by friends there too.

Sandy had some good mates and would go snorkelling and spearfishing with them on weekends, hitch hiking until he was old enough to drive. I was shy and found myself eating lunch at school alone, trying to be invisible. There were even times when I resorted to eating my hot, soggy sandwich in a toilet cubicle to avoid the cruel stares I felt in the yard. The thought makes me almost retch now but it was the only place I could hide.

We didn't understand what Mum was going through. She had left behind her stable support system; Auntie Margaret, who had nurtured and cared for her all her life, her beloved brother Don, and her neighbour and confidant, Elsie Broom. Added to these losses was the knowledge that she would never see Bryan's face on a crowded street. She was now twelve thousand miles away from him. Did she unconsciously peer at boys in Scotland who would be around his age, searching for a glimpse of his face? It was no wonder she was a mess!

Dad wasn't much help really, not being much of a talker especially if the subject was uncomfortable. He liked his routine; leaving for work early in the morning while Mum was asleep, arriving home around five pm to step into the kitchen, cuddle her from behind as she stood at the cooker, wash out his flask, wash up, eat, read the newspaper, watch TV and then go to bed. Solid, dependable, intelligent, Dad only wanted to relax after work, but she relied on him almost entirely for stimulation at the time.

Our Morrison aunts and uncles were here with their families, so Dad didn't suffer the loss and homesickness she did. Jeanie and Harry spent most Saturday nights with them, playing the Navy game of Uckers, and they often attended cabarets with the Scottish crew. Football was a great outlet for Dad, a lifelong passion. He had played a season as a professional player in Scotland when I was a baby. He had given it up because he hated the way professional games were about money and not just the love of the game. Mum was so mad, as the extra money had helped.

Dad was a founding member of the Elizabeth Thistle Soccer Club and coached the senior team for three or four years. Mum went along with all this activity, at least it got her out of the house. Most weekends were busy during the football season as she served in the makeshift canteen, but the weekdays must have dragged on endlessly for her.

When Sandy turned sixteen, he started work in 'John Martins,' a department store in Elizabeth. A few months later, I also left school as I had won a job as a clerk in a city office. Leaving school in year ten was the best option for me as, although I had enjoyed high school in Scotland, I positively hated my new school in Australia.

Sandy and I had both attended a modern secondary school in Scotland and everything, including school, seemed very backwards to us in this new land. No 'Top of the Pops' on TV, instead there was 'Bandstand' which was a bit soppy, and 'Kommotion' where people mimed the hit songs of the day. We were used to seeing the Beatles, the Stones and other famous bands on TV all the time. Fashions were also about a year behind all the latest looks the swinging sixties were offering at home.

Thankfully, the Australian music scene developed rapidly. The influx of migrants, including thousands of young people, brought a tougher edge to the music scene. Aspiring musicians such as Angus and Malcolm Young, John Swan and Jimmy Barnes arrived, quickly formed bands and took Australia by storm.

Depression continued to trouble Mum and she took a part-time job waitressing in a local hotel three nights a week, mostly to get out of the house. On the days she worked, it was my responsibility to have the dinner ready at 6.30 so we could all have dinner together. I will never forget her moods at those times. She often swept through the door with an angry huff, plopping her bag down with a bang, you could feel her anger. I realise now she would have been exhausted after her shift and the walk home.

I was very anxious at these times, not knowing how the night would end, she was so volatile when in this mood. Often Mum and Dad would begin arguing as, gentle as he was, he was no pushover. There was one night in particular that will remain imprinted on my brain forever. Mum had arrived home in a very angry mood and, when I put the dinner plates on the table, she noticed the lamb chops were a bit burnt. She started in on me with a tirade about burning the dinner and stood to take her plate to the bin, swishing past Dad on the way. As she passed him, he grabbed her and hauled her right over his knee where he proceeded to spank her bottom.

He barked that she was acting like a spoiled child and would be treated that way. Cathy, Sandy, and I took off into our bedrooms, our faces white with embarrassment and horror. Seeing Dad so angry was frightening and, as far as we knew, he had never raised his hand to her before. He was not a violent man and never hit any of us.

When the shouting ended, all was quiet for a few moments until we heard the front door slam. I heard Mum sneak home later. The incident was never spoken of; I can only imagine her terrible embarrassment and humiliation at being spanked in front of her own children.

***

As we all settled into our new lives, Mum gradually emerged from her depression. Sandy had lots of friends, including a girlfriend or two, and spent weekends down the coast at Second Valley. At seventeen, he had a car, an apprenticeship, a guitar, and a good bunch of friends. By nine, Cathy's crowd of friends was wide, and she was often out and about, busy at ballet practice or spending weekends at a cousin's or friend's house.

At fifteen, I started attending a youth club which was held at a church in the local area and finally settled into my new life. I was surprised to attract the attention of a boy named Steve, who was a year older than me, and we began to see each other regularly. It didn't take long until we were 'going steady,' as it was called in those days, and we were in love. We were both working, and he had a car, which was exciting, and we spent every moment we could together. When I was sixteen, I realised I had missed a few periods and was terrified to discover that I was pregnant.

Faced with the urgent need to take some action, I decided to run away with Steve rather than face my parents. I couldn't bear to see their disappointed looks, let alone face their anger. I was also terrified they might send me to a mother and baby home where my baby would be taken away as had happened to another girl I knew.

I spilled the news to Sandy the night before I disappeared. He didn't say very much so I'm not sure how he felt, but I told him I was going to the flat Steve shared with another guy. Leaving a note under my pillow, I snuck out of the house under the darkness of night.

Seeing my bed was empty the next day, Mum became hysterical. Sandy had promised me he wouldn't tell anyone where I was going, and he kept his word, but my parents suspected that he knew. Dad finally lost patience and told him to go to me and tell me to come home, 'or else.' I knew that I would have to face the music. Sheepishly, we slunk into the house to face the music; my knees were shaking, and I felt so sick.

Dad gave me such a disappointed look and, ignoring Steve, said *"Go to your mother"* to me. He rarely raised his voice, but we all knew that dangerous, quiet tone which indicated the depth of his anger. My legs almost gave way and I sagged into Mum's arms, her unconditional love offering me sanctuary. We both sobbed quietly for a while and clung together.

When I was able to stop crying long enough to speak, I blurted out *"I want to keep my baby"*! Mum stroked my hair and, without hesitation, said *"Of course you can!"* Those sweet, sweet words! I didn't know at that time she had suffered the kind of loss that I had been imagining and would never have allowed her own daughters to suffer the way she did.

Although my parents didn't want us to marry as we were so young, they eventually agreed, and we married a month later. The reception was held in our tiny kitchen and turned into a typical Morrison family party, with singing and laughter. I don't think Steve's parents knew quite what to do with themselves. On October the fifteenth 1969, after a long and difficult labour, a beautiful little baby girl named Sandra was placed into my arms and my heart just melted.

I stared in amazement at her perfect little face all day, but Steve had to wait until visiting hours to meet his daughter. Husbands were not allowed in the delivery suite in those days; we said goodbye to them at the hospital doors and I had faced the terrifying experience all alone.

Mum and Dad fell in love with their granddaughter instantly. Twenty years later, Mum wrote, "I didn't know how I would feel as a grandma but as soon as I saw her, I was so proud of her and love for her just flowed right through me." She always said later that her heart had grown larger and richer with the arrival of each of her fourteen grandchildren.

***

The next four years passed quickly, and during that time Mum and Dad took the gigantic step of buying their own home, something that had been impossible for the likes of us in Scotland. I was devastated when my marriage broke down and I moved home with little Sandra in tow.

We children always knew we would be welcomed home any time, our parents were incredibly supportive. I seriously don't know what I would have done without them. Mum looked after Sandra, who was a toddler at the time, and I quickly found a factory job. She really enjoyed having Sandra around, they would giggle and play games together all day. As soon as I came home, the responsibilities switched to me, which was good; Mum never overstepped by taking my place. Caring for her little granddaughter was good for Mum, and she was the most brilliant grandma as long as she remained well.

Sadly, she still suffered from illness and depression from time to time, and sometimes her dark moods were extremely debilitating, often lasting for months. I remember my new boyfriend, Edgell, buying me lots of little miniature bottles of Scotch Whisky, which I was collecting to decorate the bedroom that Sandra, Cathy, and I shared.

One day, I noticed some mould growing on one of the bottles and was shocked to find that it was filled with cold tea, and all the others proved to be the same. When I asked the family if they knew anything about it, Mum was deeply ashamed to confess that she had been drinking them to help her cope when she was at her lowest ebb. Usually a sherry and lemonade person, she must have been terribly desperate.

***

Sandy married his girlfriend Maria, and they had three boys in quick succession. He continued to play guitar, switching to bass, and played with a number of bands. They bought a lovely old cottage in Kapunda, a country town to the north of Elizabeth and started renovating it.

Cathy completed her training as a nurse and headed off with her boyfriend, John, to travel around Australia. Edgell and I built a house together and married in December 1975. We were keen to add to the family and soon welcomed three more perfect children into our brood, Rebecca, Michal and Ian.

Having so many grandchildren filled my parents' lives with love. This was especially true for Mum, who had prayed to live long enough to see her children grow up, and here she was, surrounded by the joy of grandchildren.

The grandchildren called Dad 'Papa' and Mum 'Grandma,' 'gramma' or, as they grew older, 'grams.' She was always up for a bit of a lark with them joining in with their many fantasies. As they grew, they sometimes called her 'Supergran,' with Michal proudly proclaiming he would take her to the moon one day. She would have a go at anything, even trying on Cathy's boys' inline skates once, one scary moment I can assure you.

She was a loving and patient grandmother but had clear boundaries in place, even in the midst of fun, and didn't take any nonsense. The grandchildren often speak fondly of having sleepovers at Grandma's where they slept on the sofa, and enjoyed their favourite breakfast cereal, usually forbidden at home.

Rebecca remembers one particular evening when she was a young teen. She was bemoaning the fact that her wardrobe was too young for her and 'Grams' opened hers. The next hour was spent making up outfits, with fashion lessons on how to make even a small wardrobe work for you. In particular, she learned how to add clip-on earrings to the front of plain shoes to change their look. How clever.

The years hadn't changed Dad; in his early fifties, he was as fit and slim as ever and enjoyed seeing us all when we came to visit, which was often. He played golf on weekends with Harry and Edgell and often came to watch Michal and Ian play soccer, the game he loved so much. He and Mum bought a block of land in the seaside town of Port Elliot with Jeanie and Harry and spent many weekends working on a beach shack they were building. Life was looking grand as they eagerly looked forward to Dad's retirement; as a war veteran, he could receive an aged pension at sixty.

CHAPTER TWENTY THREE

1978 - 1980

Edgell and I often popped in to see my parents on a Sunday afternoon. One Sunday, after chatting for a while, Dad said he wasn't feeling well. On closer examination, we could see that he looked terrible and thought he might be coming down with the flu. Unusually, he decided to go and rest for a while. This was quite frightening as he had never been one to be ill and we were rather worried.

Over the next thirty minutes it became obvious his condition was getting worse and he needed to see a doctor. I called the locum service, but waited in vain for one, despite calling back after an hour. Edgell took control and convinced Mum that he should just take Dad to hospital. We practically had to carry him to the car, and they screeched off as soon as Mum jumped in. The children and I waited nervously for news, knowing something dreadful was wrong. I managed to get a message to Cathy in New South Wales, and she drove alone all night to get home.

Thank God Edgell made the decision to go to hospital because Dad had suffered a major heart attack. His heart stopped as he lay on the gurney and Mum stood by him, squeezing his hand, and begging him not to leave her. Another attack followed and while they worked to resuscitate him, Mum was shoved aside. Like a thunderbolt, came the realisation that her love for him in her very soul was so deep and strong that she knew she couldn't live without him. He just couldn't die!

Dad said later that he heard Mum talking to him while he lay there and, although he didn't want to come back, he knew he had to for her sake. A heart attack was unbelievable to us as Dad was reasonably fit, never ill, and only fifty-two years old. He was a smoker though, rolling his own ciggies took him ages. They often would go out while they stuck to his lower lip and stay there for ages, so he wasn't a heavy smoker.

After many weeks in hospital, Dad made a good recovery, although his heart was left with bad scarring and he was depressed for a few months, thinking his life was virtually over. However, his good nature returned, along with his strength, and he eventually went back to work. He worked with Edgell installing industrial fire sprinkler systems in commercial buildings, so he was keeping quite fit and remained as trim as ever. He gave up smoking his famous 'rollies' and appeared to be back to his old self, although he now needed daily medication.

Life went on as it generally does, and after such a terrible fright, Mum and Dad's relationship strengthened; there was a palpable peacefulness surrounding them now. They borrowed a tent and enjoyed a lovely holiday by the sea in Port Lincoln, they were like young lovers.

Dad even organised a surprise holiday to Kangaroo Island, which was unheard of, as he had never organised anything like that in his life. Mum was amazed and moved by his gesture, and they enjoyed a fabulous time. It was as though their love had been rekindled and they were enjoying life to the full. They continued to be wonderful grandparents and loved their grandchildren deeply.

***

After travelling through the Eastern States of Australia for a couple of years, Cathy and John married and settled in Newcastle, New South Wales, where John was working. His job was more permanent than the fruit picking or casual work they had been relying on. Cathy called home weekly and, early in April 1978, happily announced that she and John would soon be adding to the growing brood of grandchildren.

A few days before Christmas, I picked up the phone to hear the beeps of an interstate call. Expecting to hear John's voice saying my sister was in labour, I was shocked to hear Cathy's voice instead. She was shouting hysterically down the line at me, and I could hardly understand what she was saying. I heard the crack of thunder in the background and torrential rain pelting on their roof. The phone line crackled ominously.

I eventually understood what she was trying to say: they had just heard that their precious baby had Hydrocephalus and was not expected to live. The doctors also said that if the baby did survive, it would be severely disabled due to brain damage. No wonder she was so distraught! Another crack of lightning sizzled down the line and the phone went dead in my hand. Shocked, I called Mum straight away and we cried together, both feeling totally helpless with Cathy so far away.

All Mum wanted to do was get to her baby girl straightaway. When I hung up from Mum, I paced around the house for several hours with my mind in a turmoil. Edgell came home from work, and I burst into tears. When I explained why, he immediately said I should go to her straight after Christmas.

This meant using all the money we had to see us through the four-week holiday break, but he didn't care and booked the tickets straight away. The strangest thing happened that Christmas Eve, when Michal, Edgell's father came for dinner. He handed me an envelope containing $500, the exact cost of the airfares. He had never done anything like that before and didn't yet know about Cathy's baby. It was the only time he ever felt to give us money, beyond the $5 he presented each of us, carefully enclosed in blank Christmas cards, every year.

Mum and I herded the children on to a plane and flew to Newcastle on Boxing Day. Having the children to organise was a blessing as keeping them amused on the two flights kept us too busy to think a lot.

Mum dissolved into tears the moment she saw Cathy: always so petite, she had ballooned with the pregnancy, even her legs and ankles were swollen. The next few weeks were trying for everyone, Cathy and John most of all. Mum was amazing, mucking in to care for the kids, despite sleeping only a few hours a night. She slept on the sofa, and the children and I slept on the floor beside her. Mostly though, it was sorrow and anxiety keeping her awake.

We watched the baby moving in Cathy's belly and felt for its little head and feet when it moved around, praying that the doctors would be proven wrong. As the baby's due date came and went, the waiting became even more difficult. We tried to make it a special time. We could hardly keep the children cooped up in the tiny flat and went to the pool or the shopping centre when we were able to. It helped to get out of the stifling heat of the flat for a while and I know that Cathy, as usual, did her best to make it a fun time for the kids. With the baby being overdue, it was as if Cathy was holding on to this little one with all her might. However, on the night of the fifteenth of January, she was admitted for an induction.

The next day, Mum and I waited anxiously for news while trying to keep the kids entertained. Our nerves were jangling, and we each took turns to hover by the phone while the other played with the children. The call came and I picked it up, Mum running to sit beside me and listen in. John was choking back sobs while attempting to say their baby son was born dead. Mum burst into tears. Sobbing, she asked him to hold Cathy tight for her until we could get to the hospital. They named him Sam.

Later, when John arrived home, Mum grabbed him and held him tight, I joined in after a moment and we all cried together. After calling his parents, he drove us in to see Cathy. Cruelly, we found that she had been placed in a private room within the maternity section, with the sound of crying babies constantly in the background. Mum, only too aware of the pain Cathy must have been feeling, sat and held her, saying nothing as she listened to her daughter sob. I stood by with the children and cried silent tears, feeling so helpless.

Cathy and John were not offered any counselling, I'm not sure any bereaved parents did in those days and no funeral was held. They were told there would be an autopsy and eventual burial in the stillborn section of the local cemetery. She was discharged with the callous advice to move on and try again. It was terrible.

Leaving for home a week later, Mum and I felt as though we were leaving Cathy to the wolves, and we cried hot salty tears as we boarded the plane. We didn't speak much on the flight home, I felt shell shocked and so did Mum. Seeing Dad and Edgell at the airport after four weeks apart was good and soothed our hearts a little.

Mum missed Cathy more than ever now and worried about how she was coping with the loss of Sam. They spoke on the phone often, but Mum couldn't help wishing Cathy and John would come home again. Thankfully, they returned to Adelaide in July, so we were all together again, and Mum's smile returned.

I now felt closer to my little sister than ever before and saw her whenever I could, but she was working and also helping on John's parent's farm. Since Sam's birth, they had been trying for another baby, but the waiting went on and on.

I remember Cathy coming to visit me in hospital when my youngest son Ian was born in 1980. She tried hard to be happy for me, not letting her pain show, but I felt so sad for her as she sat next to my baby; her own arms achingly empty. Unknown to anyone, least of all Cathy herself, there was a little blessing already growing inside her. This time, things were very different, and she gave birth to a beautiful, healthy baby boy eight months later. They gave him the name, Joseph, meaning "Jehovah will add."

CHAPTER TWENTY FOUR

1980 – 1988

In December 1983, Dad didn't appear to be his usual, easy-going self. He fainted at work one day, and after Edgell drove him home, Mum immediately insisted he see his heart specialist. After his appointment, Dad said that the doctor was happy with his health, and everything was fine. He was looking forward to the Christmas holidays, the four-week holiday beckoned, offering family times and weeks in the beach shack.

Around this time, Dad started an argument with Edgell on the way home from work. He also said some hurtful things to Cathy and John. His behaviour was totally out of character. He had always been the solid, peaceful presence in the family but now he became particularly irritable; it was a strange time.

Christmas arrived, and we enjoyed some precious time at Mum and Dad's with the whole family. We all crowded around the table loading our plates with delicious food before sitting down wherever we could to eat. The table was too small for fifteen people to fit around. Afterwards we relaxed and chatted while Dad played records on his precious radiogram. John and Cathy's two boys were jumping with joy to be leaving for a camping holiday the following day, and we all looked forward to the holiday period ahead.

We had never really entertained the thought of losing Dad, but a few days later, the phone woke us early in the morning. It was the 29th of December 1983, and my world crashed around me. I rushed to the phone. Mum was sobbing down the line, and between her gasps for breath I eventually worked out that she was saying my Dad was still in bed, but she couldn't wake him up. Shocked, I told her to go to the neighbour next door to wait and we would be there right away. I crashed the phone back in its cradle and ran to Edgell, sobbing. As the children were still asleep, he went by himself and I paced around the silent house, wringing my hands, tears streaming unheeded down my face.

Edgell found my beautiful Dad's body still in bed. When he called me with the news we had suspected, I phoned Sandy's workplace, and the caravan park where Cathy and her family were staying, leaving messages to call me urgently. This couldn't be happening! In a daze, I went about the morning, getting the children up and fed. Edgell brought Mum to our house, she was alternating between acting like a zombie and frantic activity. That afternoon, Sandy arrived and later that night, Cathy did too. We were together again, united by our loss.

We had no idea how to arrange a funeral, but we did our best. Cathy, Edgell and I went into a room to view Dad's body. I stopped short at the door, saying *"This is the wrong room, that's not Dad."* I couldn't believe the empty shell before me was him, besides they had combed his hair all wrong. This weird experience led me to question where a person's essence went after death, surely they couldn't just cease to be, as though they had never existed at all?

We muddled through the arrangements, but I wish we had been able to give Dad a funeral more worthy of the kind, funny, peaceful man he was. The funeral chapel was full to overflowing with family, friends, and work colleagues. Dad had lived a good, though short, life. He was well loved and respected and knowing how much he meant to people outside the family brought us some small comfort.

***

As Mum was an absolute mess, she stayed with us for about four weeks after Dad died. When she felt well enough to go home, fourteen-year-old Sandra insisted she go with her, and she stayed until the new school year started. We all hoped the company would help Mum in her time of deep grief. Over the following months, Mum's sorrow was so overwhelming that it consumed her.

Cathy and I took turns to visit her every day, knowing that, when we arrived, we would have to get her out of bed. We would talk with her over a cuppa, sometimes making her smile with stories of the children, but we knew she would head straight back to bed when we left. She was so unhappy and lost without Dad, and her spirit diminished in a way we had never seen before. We knew we had to help Mum, so we did as she always told us and 'pulled up our socks and got on with it' leaving our own grief on the back burner. I realised later that I was so angry without knowing who to direct my fury at. I chose Dad's doctor, who must be to blame of course and, when I saw him about six months later, I had to stop myself from shouting at him.

Over the next six months, we tried to get Mum interested in things, anything really, to get her out of the house and meeting people. How little we understood her grief! Macramé class was Cathy's great idea, but that lasted only a few weeks before she gave up. We started sewing classes together, but they only lasted about ten weeks.

Mum had relied on Dad and her children and had no outside interests to sustain her. Her health deteriorated quickly, and she suffered from many seemingly unrelated complaints such as bleeding of the bowel, phlebitis, and deep vein thrombosis. At one stage, she became dreadfully ill with toxic shock, and was given only a ten percent chance of survival. We constantly worried about her, all alone in the house.

Thankfully, around eighteen months later, Mum's health picked up enough to enable her to pick up our youngest son, Ian, from kindergarten, three mornings a week. This was a huge undertaking and meant I had to run around picking her up and dropping her off before and after work, but the hassle was worth it to see the light coming back into her eyes. She loved spending time collecting Ian at noon and walking him back to my house, usually a very slow trip as there were many adventures on the way.

She loved seeing all the children and played silly games with them when she stayed long enough for dinner, and her health continued to improve. However, when school started the following year, she felt lonely and useless once again. Cathy and I picked her up every Thursday, and would spend the whole day with her, shopping, having lunch and paying bills. We continued to pop in as often as possible, but she soon slipped back into ill health and depression.

Sandy's marriage to Maria sadly ended and he purchased some land interstate, moving there to build a new home. Over the next few years, whenever she was well enough, Mum would brave the trip to visit him. I say 'brave' because she had to adapt a great deal to cope with his lifestyle, however she was such a great sport. He had no 'mod cons' in his temporary shelter, no electricity or running water, and candles were the only way to light the way to bed at night. Coping with these inconveniences was the price she happily paid to see her son and his family, and she made the best of things.

However, on what would become her last trip there, she became very ill and was hospitalised. When she was sufficiently recovered, she flew home and tried to make the best of living alone again, struggling with depression and ill health. With so much time alone, her memories and unresolved traumas plagued her leaving her with unresolved anger and guilt.

***

Cathy and John became Christians and developed a deep faith in God. Cathy had been speaking with Mum, encouraging her to study the Bible for herself, believing strongly that Mum would find healing with God's help, but she resisted. She didn't believe she could be forgiven for 'giving her son away,' and she certainly was not going to forgive her father for his unforgiveable abuse. She would become angry with Cathy, saying again and again, "*I can't forgive.*'

However, after praying in desperation for so many years while we were children, she began to attend a woman's Bible study group and soon developed a deep yet humble faith, and accepted Christ into her heart. She started to attend the church where Edgell and I belonged, and it was there that a wise and caring minister advised her to write about her life. He explained how the process of writing could help her to let go, to release her pain, and perhaps help her to forgive herself for giving up her son for adoption. It was a regret and grief that had troubled her since she was twenty years old. He helped her to understand forgiveness, explaining that it is not a feeling, it is a decision to release yourself from the poison eating away at you from inside. She learned that holding on to the trauma of abuse and refusing to forgive those who abused her wouldn't affect them at all, but would poison her own soul.

Did she eventually forgive her father and Tommy, her rapist? I believe she did her very best to do so and was finally able to forgive herself as well. Her newfound faith and the process of writing about her life helped her in a way that didn't seem possible, and she found a freedom she hadn't known existed.

***

While Mum was living alone, she took a bad turn late one night and fainted, hitting her head on the coffee table. She lay unconscious on the living room floor and when she awoke, she found herself bleeding. She lay there for hours, unable to reach the phone, yet she somehow staggered to bed. It was terrifying for her to feel so helpless, but the scare made her look realistically at her situation and come to the important decision of selling her home.

She had a small transportable house put on the block of land behind us. The land was owned by Edgell's father, Michal, a kind and generous man who respected Mum immensely. He happily signed a 'peppercorn' lease, allowing her to live there for the rest of her life, bless him. Her new home, which she aptly named 'gingerbread cottage' was tiny but very comfortable and she loved it. With one bedroom, a bathroom and an open plan living, kitchen and dining area, she had all the room she needed.

Retaining her independence was important to her and this allowed her to be close to us, while totally independent. With a gate through the fence between us leading straight into her garden, the kids were able to visit her before and after school most days. It was perfect!

After writing her story and developing such a strong faith, Mum turned a corner in her life, and the next few years were busy. She took a counselling course and after graduation, commenced as a volunteer for 'Birthline,' a pregnancy help centre. She felt that she could make a difference to other women who were in trouble, and her non-judgemental, compassionate character, enabled her to be a wonderful counsellor.

Mum had open heart surgery to replace her faulty mitral valve and after the difficult months of recovery was off and running again, enjoying life and her family to the full. She travelled to Scotland in yet another search for Bryan and, while she was there, she registered with Jigsaw, an organisation which assists children and their birth mothers to reconnect. She left a letter that she had written to Bryan with them, and also left a copy with our cousin, Joan, who still lives in Scotland.

Her fervent hope was that eventually he would be found and would read the letter, even if he didn't want any other contact with her. We remain hopeful that one day he could learn the truth about his adoption and how much Mum loved him. She never stopped searching for him and he lived in her heart forever. Sadly, she never heard from him.

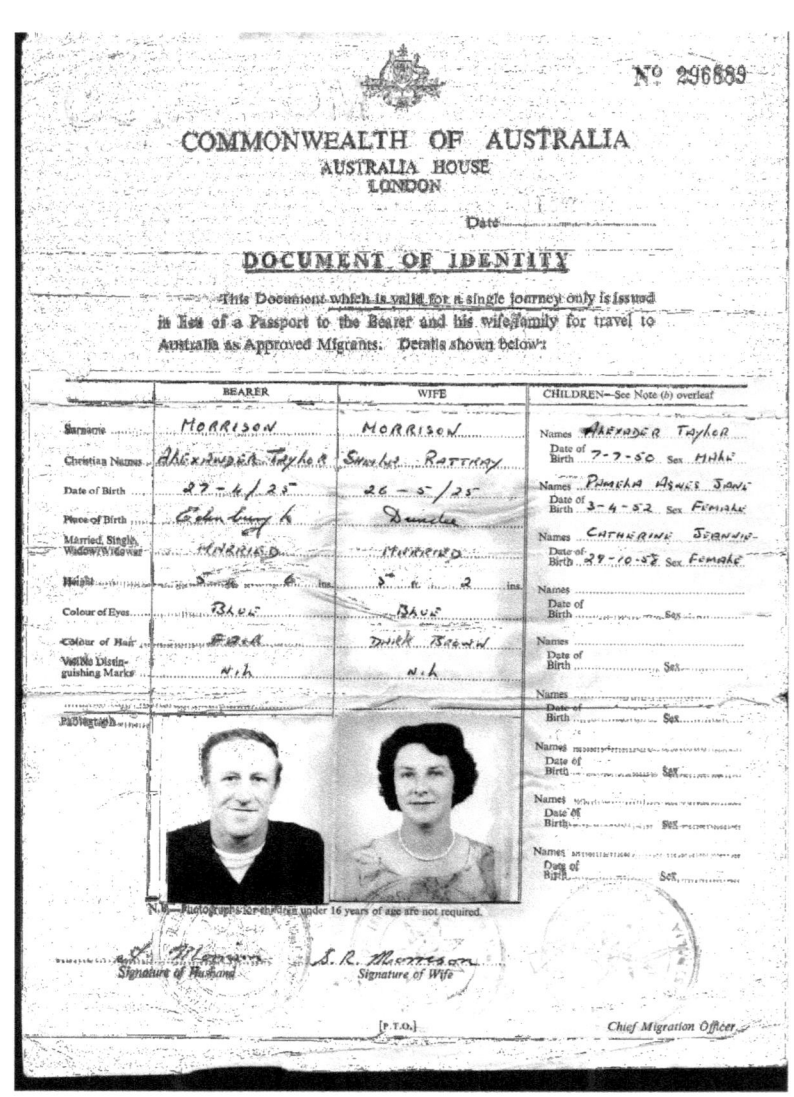

Instead of passports, we entered Australia on this document, October 31 1965

We visited many places in Edinburgh before leaving. Dad, Catherine (with her monkey Jacko), Mum, and Sandy at the zoo August 1965

Mum and Dad looking healthy and happy in our lounge room, Elizabeth Grove 1965

Dad, Mum, Cathy, and I in our backyard in Elizabeth Grove with our dog, Kym.

Cathy with friends outside the cubby house dad made from our packing crate.

Mum's tiny home, 'Gingerbread Cottage', before the garden is done

Bryan's birth certificate obtained in 1990 as Mum's search continued

Adelaide woman trying to trace her long lost son

SIR, — I am trying to trace the adopted son of a 67 year old woman who is Mrs. Sheila Morrison, 123 Stanford Road, Salisbury Heights, Adelaide 5109, South Australia.

The story is really quite tragic. Her son was born as a result of an attack on her in Edinburgh. After the birth she was taken by relatives to some office where she was told to hand over the baby and he would go to a good home. She didn't realise before she went, in that she would be leaving without her baby. She loved the child and wanted to keep him and she was absolutely devastated to lose him.

It has always been her fervent wish to trace him and this has been made more urgent by her failing health. She suffers from a ......

in her youth. I have become involved because I have gained some experience in tracing missing persons. I have previously helped others to find their missing relatives. I don't charge money, I just do it to help. I am just an ordinary wife and mother.

The child was born at the Simpson Memorial Maternity Pavilion on March 3, 1946. Sheila named him Bryan George Bell but his name was changed to William when he was adopted.

The only definite information we have on him is his date of birth, his Christian name and the fact that he was adopted in

Berwickshire by a childless couple in their thirties. They later said they were very happy with him. This letter might jog the memories of those that knew him. If I could discover his surname I could probably trace him.

Any results should be sent to me rather than Sheila. If the story does not have a happy ending I would like to shield her from that as much as possible.

I thank you in keen anticipation of your help.

MRS. WENDY GRANT,
143 Oxford St.,
Rugby,
Warks. CV21 3LZ.

Mum continued searching for her son until Alzheimers disease stopped her.

The letter Mum wrote to her son Bryan. We keep it, unopened, in hope of finding him

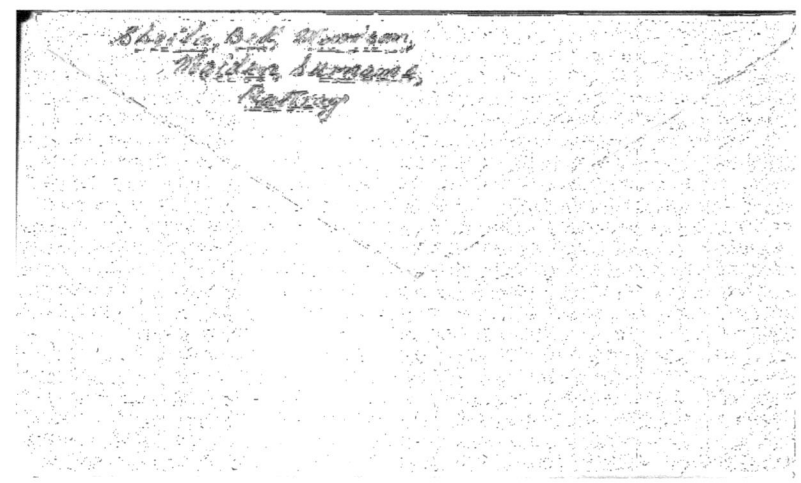

Although Mum rarely used her legal maiden surname, she wrote it at the rear of Bryan's letter

Morrison clan leave Waverley station. Sandy 2nd from left rear, Dad holding Cathy 4th from left rear, Mum next to him, Pam 2nd from right front in light coloured coat

Mum and her beloved sister Margaret 1986

Mum, Margaret and brother Don on Mum's last trip to Scotland, 1991

CHAPTER TWENTY FIVE
1988 - 1998

I remember bopping along to the Beatles song 'When I'm sixty-four' when I was fifteen years old, thinking sixty-four was indeed ancient. Ah, the folly of youth!

Mum was still sprightly at that age and had always been taken for someone at least ten years younger than she was. I remember a few times being asked if she was my older sister. However, it was when she was only sixty-four that strange incidents began to occur. She missed appointments, became lost in familiar places and couldn't work out where to catch trains or buses. Even cooking a favourite meal had become a challenge.

One day she was taking Cathy's youngest boy, Benny, to the city for the day and was waiting with him on the platform. Benny kept pulling at her hand, saying they were on the wrong platform. He was around five at the time and was adamant that he was right. Mum hushed him a few times before she began to doubt herself, and they crossed to the opposite platform. The train was arriving as they reached the platform, and as it pulled in Mum saw that he was correct.

I can only imagine her response; she must have been so embarrassed and confused. Was she beginning to think that she was going out of her mind?

Although Mum was living directly behind us, basically in our back yard, it wasn't long before her phone calls were waking us up in the middle of the night. It was obvious from her voice she was very frightened, convinced that there was someone hiding in her house or garden. After these calls, Edgell would sleepily trudge down torch in hand, and begin checking through the garden and house to find that there was no intruder.

He would then calm her down and reassure her there was no-one there before coming back to bed. On a few occasions, we were woken by a torch shining around outside our bedroom window, only to discover police officers searching our property. They were acting on Mum's frightened calls, to report intruders in her yard.

Gradually, we came to see that Mum's condition was deteriorating. We could no longer ignore or explain away her behaviour, particularly after a few perplexing confrontations between us. Now that we, her children, were adults, Mum generally avoided arguing with us, instead showing her anger by storming off, lips pursed and head up, without explaining why she was so mad. She would make herself scarce for a while until we approached her to try to clear the air; we could never stand it for long.

However, as her condition deteriorated, she became unable to follow conversations and would insert her own thoughts, words, or feelings into a situation. Misunderstandings became constant, creating havoc for everyone as we tried to understand why she was so angry or upset.

A decision was finally made to get some help from our doctor who referred her to a psychiatrist. He put her through a barrage of quizzes and puzzles, and I remember feeling terribly embarrassed for her when she failed to work many of them out. I was shocked with the frightening diagnosis of Alzheimer's disease. How could this be, I thought, she is sixty-four, not ninety.

Her mental state declined quite rapidly after the diagnosis, along with her confidence. I can only imagine how her confusion and the mistakes she made would have affected her; I sometimes see my own kids giving me knowing looks when I just can't get the right word immediately. It is frightening and embarrassing, and I now have a little understanding of how easily you can lose your confidence.

In light of her appalling diagnosis, Edgell and I decided that Mum should visit her family in Scotland before her deteriorating condition made such a trip impossible. I booked time off work to travel with her, and I have to say that in my experience, travelling with someone who is suffering from dementia is a BIG mistake! We didn't know that taking someone with dementia out of their comfort zone leads to a nightmare, for both the sufferer and the carer. From the moment we took off in the plane, she became agitated. She would regularly stand up, saying *"Well I'm off to bed then."* Each time, I would explain that we were on a plane, but she would stand up and claim that she was getting off and I would have to distract her somehow. It was a long, exhausting, terrible flight!

Our time in Scotland had a few happy moments but I was on edge the entire time. I had to watch Mum like a hawk, ready to defuse countless difficult situations following her mix-ups. Needless to say, my own mental health was affected by having to watch her constantly. I was exhausted and my final semblance of sanity went out the window on our trip home after four weeks in Scotland.

On the way home to Australia, we stopped for the night in Hong Kong. After another exhausting, frustrating flight followed by a bus ride, we finally reached our hotel room late at night. As we were so shattered, we were both looking forward to getting some sleep. Mum settled herself into our bed and snuggled up, looking ready to drift off, so I decided to run myself a bath. I sank gratefully into the warm water, a sigh of gratitude escaping from my lips, when she knocked loudly on the bathroom door. Apparently, she was going out shopping, so I clambered clumsily out of the bath, dried off quickly and climbed into bed with her, hoping to soothe her to sleep.

It wasn't to be however, and she was up and down every five minutes, pacing around the room. I became so exasperated that I decided to give her one of the mild sleeping pills she had been prescribed. An hour later, still no sleep and, remembering that the doctor had prescribed two at night, I gave her another. At one thirty am, with tears of desperation escaping my eyes from trying to get her to stay in the bloody bed, I gave her a third!

I can only claim diminished responsibility due to mental and physical exhaustion to excuse my actions! She eventually fell asleep around 2.30 but I was so wired by that time that I couldn't sleep. I reached out and took one of her pills, the first sleeping pill I had ever taken and soon fell into a dreamless state.

I was woken by the sound of people talking in the corridor and, panicking in case I had killed my mother, I turned to see if she was still alive. Thankfully, she was and, because we were leaving that day, I checked my watch. It read three fifteen. Believing it was three fifteen am, I turned to snuggle down and get more sleep when I noticed light seeping through the gap in the curtains.

Confused, I jumped up and peeked through the gap, thinking that the lights must be from streetlights. Imagine my horror when I saw the bright sunshine outside and realised it was afternoon! We were due to meet in the lobby for our bus driver to transport us to the airport at three forty-five! I shook Mum frantically, it took a while to wake her, and eventually we were both dressed. We entered the lobby - smack on time. With our luggage set before us, we sat down to wait for the driver to arrive.

Naturally, Mum was restless and stood up every time a bus drove by the plate glass windows around us. I kept explaining that the bus wasn't ours, saying *"See the Chinese writing, Mum, it can't be ours, please sit down"*. This became my constant, although rather useless, refrain. Across from our seat there was a jewellery store, right there in the lobby. The shiny jewellery caught Mum's eye and she said she was going to look in the window. As it was only about twenty feet away, I watched her walk over to the window and kept my eagle eye on her. It was a relief not to keep repeating myself for a few moments.

She was happily peering into the gleaming window when a group of jostling young people tumbled through the main doors, into the lobby. They crossed between us, chattering and laughing as they headed for the lifts, and as the last one passed, I realised that Mum was nowhere to be seen.

Thinking that she had gone inside the shop, I left our bags and rushed over to peer inside. She wasn't there! I frantically looked to my left and was horrified to see a corridor running straight into a covered market, jam packed with people. My heart racing in panic, I took off at a terrified sprint down the corridor and into the market but couldn't see her as I anxiously peered into the crowd. I ran up and down the busy aisles, pushing past people for what felt like hours but was probably only five minutes, and eventually noticed her calmly looking at the toys on display at a stall and chatting brightly with the stall holder, who looked rather bemused.

I burst into hysterical tears at that point and grabbed her in a grappling hug. We staggered back to the lobby just in time to pick up our luggage - thankfully still there - and climbed aboard the waiting bus. FYI, anyone who thinks about taking someone with Alzheimer's on an overseas holiday, DON'T, it is cruel to them and will almost kill you.

***

Taking her out of her usual surroundings exposed the reality of how far Mum's illness had progressed. Before the trip, we thought she was able to function reasonably well most of the time, with only the occasional mistake, but we now realised she had hidden the confusion from us. She was a brilliant actress. We began to see she was in danger while living alone, as she often wandered during the night. The only thing we could do to support her and keep her safe was to have her live with us. We began to alternate days of staying between Cathy's home and ours.

Between us, we were able to care for her this way, quite a 'tag team' effort. We didn't realise at the time that moving from one house to the other wasn't good for Mum. It certainly wasn't great for our respective family lives either. We all did our best to accommodate her needs, but the longer she stayed with us, the greater her symptoms were revealed.

One of the many qualities Mum had drilled into us as children was honesty. Lying was tantamount to the worst crime we could commit. Like all children, I lied at times to protect myself from being in trouble, and Mum would fix me with her 'special' look, asking, *"On your honour, did you...?"* We all knew without a doubt, that if we lied 'on our honour', the punishment would be severe if the lie was ever uncovered. This made the need to lie to her to protect her from the terrible truths she had forgotten, almost impossible. We had to lie sometimes though, for her own sake.

Often, after a shopping day or doctor's appointment, she would sit next to me in the car on the way home wringing her hands anxiously. She would ask me what time it was, and then say that she had to hurry back to make Dad's tea. Initially, I would roll my eyes surreptitiously and try to calm her, saying *"There's no need to rush, Dad's not there anymore,"* or something similar. Of course, she would cry and ask what had happened and I would tell her that he had died.

Of course, my answer would lead to questions as to how and when he had died. After saying what happened, she would be overcome with grief... fresh, painful, and raw each time. Less than thirty minutes later, I would go through the same process and watch her suffer until I learned to lie. I know Cathy did the same and throughout this time, we had to relive his death, grief and all.

Continual 3 am escape attempts, misunderstandings, arguments, tears from confused children and accidently locked bathroom doors eventually wore us down. Close encounters with fire also forced us to continually check that she hadn't turned the gas cooker on. We began to realise it was becoming too much for us all. Cathy and I were continually stressed trying to keep the cracks from showing and we started to look for a respite place to give us a desperately needed break.

We visited many nursing homes in our 'spare' time and found that some were awful. We began to despair of ever finding a suitable place. Thankfully, after searching for weeks, we found the Helping Hand centre, which was close to our homes. It felt warm and welcoming and had a key code on the exit door for safety. There were gardens all around and lovely large windows, making the rooms bright and cheerful. We felt it was the right place for Mum and were hopeful she would settle there.

Luckily, they had a respite room available, and she would be able to stay for a whole nine weeks, fully funded. We told Mum she was lucky to be going on a 'holiday' and, while we packed some clothes, we chattered on about how lovely her little 'hotel' room was and drove her there. We settled her in, placing photographs and some of her loved ornaments around the room and showed her where all the facilities were. The staff were wonderful, very welcoming, and she was quite happy with the idea of a holiday when we left.

Walking out of the sliding doors and leaving Mum behind, all alone, was one of the most difficult things I have ever done. Would she think we had abandoned her? We were haunted by our decision. Mum had been an expert at holding everything together over short visits from friends and family and we understood some of our uncles and aunties were angry about the move. This made us feel even worse, but they couldn't see how much of Mum's mind the disease had stolen.

Thankfully we were together in the nursing home decision and, although Sandy was interstate and couldn't see first-hand how much she had declined, he was fully supportive. Over the next six weeks we began to feel like ourselves again, despite some traumatic visits when we would find her sitting in her chair, all packed up and ready to go home.

As the end of the respite period loomed large, Cathy and I started to panic about the prospect of bringing Mum home again, just as she had settled in. With no upcoming permanent place available, Cathy and I often looked closely at a few of the other residents. We would comment to each other later, "Oh Mr or Mrs so and so isn't looking too well, maybe her room will be empty soon." Shameful behaviour, but we were so desperate! Thankfully, in the last week of the allotted respite period the manager called to offer Mum a permanent place. Thankfully she wouldn't even have to change rooms. In our relief, we were too ashamed to ask who had 'moved on.'

Mum's little room began to look more homely as we could now move some of her own furniture in. She had plenty of visitors with Cathy and I each popping in a few times a week, and Edgell taking her out for a drive as often as he could. He loved to give her a laugh by letting her steer the car when they were on a quiet road. She came home with us for family meals and birthdays and generally life was more relaxed.

As the best actress on the planet, Mum made some daring escapes over the following years. Although a code was needed to exit through the main doors, she often fooled visitors as they entered. She would appear to be a visitor herself and walk out with a thank you and a smile as they came through the door. She certainly didn't look old or frail and appeared very 'with it', so the incoming visitor didn't suspect a thing. I received more than a few calls at work from her. She would call from a phone box, saying she didn't know where she was. Sometimes, she would hop on the bus which stopped near the nursing home and get off at any shopping centre it passed.

She would wander around happily for a while before realising that she was lost. How terrifying it must have been for her to look around and see nothing familiar. Strangely, she still remembered my work phone number which was a blessing. She lived at the Helping Hand centre for about four years before her escapades became much too dangerous. Managing her behaviour had also become more difficult, as she often wandered in and out of the other resident's rooms taking anything she liked.

Thankfully, a place was found in the secure dementia unit in the centre where Cathy worked as a palliative care nurse. Although this was further away, I still managed to visit a couple of times a week and Cathy often popped in after her shifts. Despite seeing us a lot, she began to forget who we were and would sometimes introduce us to the staff as her friends. She was quite happy there once she had settled in; she was becoming more childlike, and we were happy that she was well cared for in a safe place.

I have the happiest memories of visiting her and entering the unit's double doors, only to see her at the other end of the corridor look up to see who it was. She would smile and open her arms wide for me to cuddle into her. Whether she knew who I was or not, her cuddles soothed me and blessed me with her love.

One day, Sandy made the long drive down to Adelaide for a visit. All four of us were sitting at a table chatting one day and Mum kept sending angry glances his way, much to our confusion. Eventually she spoke and, sending a withering glance his way, accused him of looking like her son. We three couldn't help laughing, which made Mum even more cross.

CHAPTER TWENTY SIX

1997

Since becoming adults, Cathy and I had ferried Mum around to her medical appointments and the weekly grocery shopping. Following Dad's death she was on her own, and gradually became even more reliant on us. We were pretty much 'on-call', ready to step in at a moment's notice, especially when she was ill. We had spent innumerable hours in hospitals or sitting in doctor's waiting rooms, often trying to keep our tired children amused and quiet.

Over her entire life, despite many close calls with the grim reaper, she would beat the odds and pull through. Our favourite saying at these times became *"That's Mum, you couldn't kill her with an axe."* We were accustomed to the drama of it all.

One cold evening in July 1997, we didn't 'jump to' as we had done in the past when a phone call came summonsing us to hospital. Mum was ill with dreadful stomach pains. Strangely, Cathy and I finished what we had been doing prior to the call before leaving home. I finished having dinner with my family, and she finished a heavy gardening task in the vegetable plot.

We both arrived at the hospital at the same time and looked at each other, aware of our weird behaviour, before heading inside. On reflection, perhaps we both realised somewhere inside ourselves just how serious this illness would be, and that it would lead to a final goodbye. Maybe we just needed some space to process this.

We were told that Mum was in a bad way, there was a hole in her stomach, allowing acid to seep through, causing the intense pain. The doctors worked to stabilise her enough for surgery and she was whisked away. We sat in the drab waiting area outside theatre, wondering how this night would end, when a young doctor dashed in clutching some forms to be signed. He asked us if it was Mum's wish that she be resuscitated if her heart gave up its long fight during surgery. In complete unison, we said *"no."* As he hurried from the room, we looked at each other in shock; we had never discussed this with Mum but had both instantly concluded that she would not wish to be brought back if God decided to take her that night.

The surgery went well, the hole in her stomach was repaired and strengthened with mesh, and a biopsy taken. A week later, the doctor gave us the devastating news that the hole had been caused by an aggressive cancer. Surgery was not an option they could consider, and any treatment regime would only buy her a little time. It would have been terribly cruel to put her through it and together, we decided to keep her as comfortable as possible for whatever time remained to her.

When she returned to the home, she soon settled in again and was mostly pain free. Watching her over the next few months as she dissolved away before our eyes, becoming quite skeletal, was truly devastating. Nevertheless, it still did my heart good every time she gave me a bright smile when I visited her. I knew she didn't know who I was but that didn't matter to me.

Her condition became terminal within three months of her diagnosis, and she was moved to the hospice unit. Although she was conscious, she seemed to take the move in her stride. Within weeks, she became bedridden, and often drifted in and out of sleep. Sandy flew down, and over the next week or so, our vision narrowed to her room only, and time seemed to stop. It felt as though the outside world had almost ceased to exist.

Cathy, Sandy and I were with her constantly. We played music in the room, and I wonder what she thought of our music choice. It was Celtic, peaceful and quite haunting, but perhaps she would have preferred the Glen Miller orchestra. We used essential oils to perfume the air gently. We read quietly, shared stories and sometimes cracked jokes, leading us to collapse in fits of laughter; she would have loved that. It was almost impossible for Sandy and Cathy to be in the same room at any time without jokes and laughter flying around. It felt right. It felt like love.

Cathy and I took turns to sleep in the chair next to her bed each night and Sandy stayed all day, leaving only after dark. Edgell came in daily, and one evening brought his father to visit. He and Mum had shared an affinity born of respect and affection. When he gently spoke to her, she opened her eyes and thanked him. He left with tears clouding his eyes.

I felt so privileged to be with Mum during her last days on earth and, strange though it may be to say, it was a blessed time! After the love and care that she had given me as I grew up, and the years spent helping her in return, it felt right to be alongside her 'til the end. I began to understand in those almost holy days that death is as sacred as birth. Her room was infused with reverence and love.

Thank goodness for Cathy. She is an incredible, caring, nurse who knew how to keep a patient comfortable. We swabbed Mum's mouth with lemon water when it appeared dry. We bathed her with scented water before wrapping her with warm, soft towels. What a privilege it was to be able to care for her in such an intimate way. Watching her with a compassionate, yet clinical eye, for the slightest grimace of discomfort or pain, Cathy was quick to act. I don't know how she was able to keep herself from breaking down, I guess she had to put on her professional 'hat' at times.

Many of her beloved grandchildren were able to visit in those precious, final days, spreading themselves and their love around the room, and we were amazed when sometimes her fog cleared, and she realised their presence. Over her last few days, she experienced a few astoundingly lucid moments. In those moments, she would open her eyes and reach for the hand of whomever of her children was sitting closest to her.

I remember the intense look she had summoned from somewhere within when she reached for my hand and, with pure simplicity, breathed *"I love you..."* Those final words echoed inside my heart the last words she used to say at night, *"Always remember I love you"*... I dissolved into tears. We were each blessed by her in this way before she closed her tired eyes, job done, and faded into a coma.

***

Mum finally abandoned her lifelong fight to survive and slipped away peacefully on the 27th of October 1997, aged seventy-two. Our beautiful mother left this world surrounded by the three children who were privileged to have been raised by her. The woman who had begged God to make sure she lived long enough to see her children grow up, discarded her earthly shell after living a life of steely determination, courage, and compassion, sometimes hanging on to those characteristics by the slimmest of threads.

She had not only lived long enough to raise three strong children but was also able to enjoy being surrounded by her loving grandchildren whom she treasured so much. Before Alzheimer's stole a large part of her mind, she also was delighted to meet two great-grandsons, Damian, and Shannon. Her desperate prayers as a young mother were answered more abundantly than she could possibly have imagined.

Mum's funeral was a joyous affair. Although the tears flowed freely, there was also a great deal of laughter in the church that day. Her beautiful eulogy was delivered by a delightful young man, Mark, who was a member of our church. We asked him because Mum had become quite close to him when she was still able to attend services. She seemed to sense an innate goodness within him. They would often be seen cackling over a joke or two, and she sometimes called him her 'boyfriend'; much to everyone's bewilderment, especially his patient wife.

Her sense of humour and ability to see the funny side of life remained one of her brightest qualities until the end.

At the cemetery, a piper played 'Amazing Grace', her favourite hymn, as she was carried to her final resting place. The haunting sound almost breaking my resolve not to break down completely. Cathy and I were determined to share in bearing Mum's coffin to her final resting place. After carrying her for so long, we wanted to honour her to the last; that break from tradition raised a few eyebrows, I can tell you! I'll never forget the shock of feeling how heavy her casket was, she had been so frail and tiny at the end.

***

Writing my mother's story has given me the opportunity to reflect on who she was, and what she means to me still. Being loved and raised by her taught me so much. She loved fiercely and with genuine compassion. She showed me how to forgive others, and myself. One of her many sayings, which made me roll my eyes when I was young, was "There but for the grace of God, go I". I miss her sayings. Those timeless words of wisdom.

She instilled in me the kind of self-respect I would need to navigate this sometimes harsh world and to respect others, even though I may dislike or disagree with them.

Her insistence on honesty is embedded so deeply inside me that it can cause me a little stress at times. I try hard to remain tactful while being honest, a tricky task!

The unconditional love she modelled for me taught me how to love my own children. This has never been more apparent than the times I have watched on as each of my four kids have travelled along difficult paths, not necessarily the paths I would have chosen for them. They know I will be there for them until I take my last breath.

The memories I have of laughing with Mum until I couldn't breathe are ones I especially cherish. Cathy and I, along with our large brood of children took Mum shopping every Thursday. Those days would lead to so many opportunities to laugh until we cried, leaving me with memories I'll treasure forever. I don't know how Mum coped with the madness sometimes, we put her through so much: running out of petrol, medical emergencies, lost children, Mum falling out of car doors etc. On one occasion, she jammed her finger in the door of Cathy's combi van and ran alongside saying... "my finger, my finger". In her haste to get home, Cathy didn't notice for a few moments. This led to yet another hospital visit. Mum took it all in her stride!

She showed me how to have the courage to grab at every opportunity to be silly, to mess about, and to laugh at the absurd. This lesson is never more important to me than when everything in my life seems to be crashing around me.

I particularly remember shopping one day when our family had been going through a very difficult time financially. Mum noticed me replacing several grocery items back on the shelves. She quietly passed me a $20 note, whispering *"this is not a loan"*. I burst into tears. She put her arm around my shoulders and squeezed until we were both consumed with laughter, silly tears streaming down both faces.

Mum's resilience was extraordinary. She survived more trauma than the majority of people suffer in their lifetime. As children, we watched on as she was dragged down into her own private hell, time and time again. The lesson for us was witnessing her refusal to give up; always 'pulling her socks up and getting on with it'.

I'm sure that all mothers, certainly including me, grapple with the problem of knowing how to be a good mother. I have struggled and strived at times to get it right, only to blame myself when I've fallen short of my own expectations. None of us are perfect.

Perhaps being a good mother is as simple as encircling your children with unconditional love, ensuring that they know it's OK not to be OK...

If that is the key, and I believe it is, I know without a doubt that my mother, Sheila, got it just right.

Sheila's story would be incomplete without a few
words from my siblings, Sandy and Cathy, who
were also blessed to have been raised by her.

The poem Sandy has written is at the front
of this book, and Cathy has shared a few
memories and lessons on the following page.

LESSONS FROM MY MOTHER, BY CATHY

I learned so much from mum, she was a strong woman, deeply affected by her experiences as a child and a young woman. Nevertheless, she was determined to choose love for her children over bitterness from her past. There are so many lessons she gave me; the following are just a few...

She taught me to love my children unconditionally.
I was rather headstrong in my younger years and at one stage got into a bit of trouble which resulted in my having to attend court with my parents. Dad was unable to go so mum had to face this alone. I was aware that she was very upset about the behaviour that brought me here, yet she held her head high and stood by my side and loved me through it all. I will never forget the feeling of her unconditional love for me.

She taught me to be patient with my children.
When I was in primary school, Pamela and Sandy were much older than me so mum was the person I would constantly talk to. When I came home from school, I would plop down on the high stool next to the cooker and yabber on and on and

on, while she made dinner. She would just listen to me and appear interested.

She would play along when I was pretending to be a nurse. I would come home from school with my cardigan draped across my shoulders, like a nurse's cape, and say, "sorry I can't talk today I am on duty". I would then hurry off to tend to my patients who were my dolls, lined up in their little beds. She would become part of my game, joining in with my imagination. She never made me feel silly, I really loved that about her.

She taught me resilience.
When I was going through rough times, she would say "you've never died a winter yet". In other words, I had come through life this far and could get through anything so I should never give up. She taught me ownership of my own choices, and to never feel sorry for myself.

She never pitied herself despite times of deep sadness following the abuse she had experienced. She very much owned her own feelings and was determined to avoid projecting them onto anyone else. She always said that no matter how we felt, we shouldn't make others' lives miserable just because we were experiencing a rough time.

She taught me to love my siblings.
Mum's love for her sister Margaret and her other siblings taught me to love my brother and sister (even when they threaten to 'dob' me in for something).

A wise woman once said to me that 'your siblings are a gift from your parents to you'. How true this is, I have been blessed with a brother and sister and we share a deep love for each other.

She taught me that even the most horrific things can be forgiven.
Before mum became a Christian, her hatred for her father was intense. In my early teens, I watched on eagerly as mum opened a letter from Scotland, expecting news from 'home'. She read the short letter silently and glanced up with a blank face saying, "my father has died". I stared at her, waiting for a reaction. There was no emotion on her face, it was blank. She folded the letter and placed it on the table, then continued with her housework as though nothing had happened. I will never forget my shock; she really hated him and was glad he had gone! Mum would never have been able to forgive her father if she had not experienced the love of Jesus. His gentle way of leading her through the pain to a place of forgiveness freed her from the weight of hatred.

***

As I look back and talk with Pamela and Sandy, I realise that we each see our mother in different ways. It is only now, as I am older myself, that I can catch a glimpse of her as a woman in her own right, apart from my childhood eyes. I am so grateful to have had the chance to know her and be loved by her.

I am greatly indebted to my dear sister Pamela for writing this book. I am so grateful for the time, the tears and endurance she has gone through in writing this great story of our brave mother. I love you, dear sister.

ACKNOWLEDGMENTS

My goodness, how on earth do I say thank you to all the people who have helped me reach this point? Firstly, I thank my mother, Sheila. I was blessed to be raised by you, I will never forget your deep, tough love and your wise sayings.

To my children, Sandra, Rebecca, Michal, and Ian, thank you, I love you always and forever and pray this book does justice to your amazing Grandma's story. My beautiful grandchildren and greatgrandchildren, take courage from reading this book, you share Grandma's genes.

It is an honour to have been supported and encouraged along each step of the journey by many friends. Thank you to my dearest friend Joy in particular; you know what for. To my TafeSA friendship group, thanks for the laughs and genuine care, it means so much to me. To my family far and wide, your gentle nudges have kept me going through hard times.

To those who gladly read some very early drafts, Tim and Ali, a heartfelt thank you for not being too harsh. To my Beta readers, I am indebted to you for your gentle suggestions and for giving up your precious time to read my final draft (s): Jo,

Matt, Ian, Michal, Edgell, Cathy and Ali, your advice has helped me to 'show - not tell'. Rebecca, I can't thank you enough for your fabulous cover ideas and marketing advice. Sandra, your encouragement and support has meant so much to me.

To my editor, Lynne Lloyd, lloydmosspublishing.com, thank you for your calm guidance and understanding. The Playford Writing group have helped immensely; thank you for your belief in this story. Special thanks to Tiara King for all the wonderful publishing information and support. Sarah Nelson, thanks for leading our group and providing a safe space to share our work and support each other.

Thank you to my Scottish cousins, especially Joan, Anne and David, for the information you have generously provided and your ongoing encouragement. Also, special thanks for the abundant Scottish hospitality over the years, you are amazing! Thank you to the Salvation Army who provided my grandmother's records.

My brother Sandy and sister Cathy, thank you for believing that I could write this book. I treasure our childhood memories and the special love we share.

To my beloved husband Edgell, I thank you from the bottom of my heart for supporting me, even when I've been so focussed that I've deserted you. Thank you for truly caring for my mother, I could not have written her story without you. Thanks for bringing cups of tea, wine, gin or whatever on so many long writing days and for the 'debriefs'. You believed in me when I doubted myself. Now it's time to scratch those itchy feet my love, I love you eternally.

GLOSSARY

SCOTS WORD	TRANSLATION
a'	All
Awfie	Awful
Aye	Yes
Bairn	Child or infant
Banns	Marriage license
Beasties	Insects
Ben	Through
Besom	Literally a broom, but also 'sassy' or 'bitch.
Bobby	Police Officer
Coos	Cows
Darning	A difficult mending skill with a weaving effect.
Dinnae	Don't
Doon	Down
Faither	Father
Gie'	Give
Git	Get
Hen	Darling, pet, love, honey etc.
Hogmanay	Scottish New Year's Eve
Hoose	House
Messages	Shopping
Noo	Now
Och	Oh!
Oot	Out
Pinny	Apron
Rag and bone man	Purchaser of rags, bones and other items, etc. He travelled the streets in a horse and cart, ringing a bell and loudly calling "rags and bones"!
Wee	Small
Willnae	Will not
Withoot	Without
Ye	You
Yersel	Yourself
Yon	That

www.ingramcontent.com/pod-product-compliance
Lightning Source LLC
Chambersburg PA
CBHW040240010526
44107CB00065B/2809